Radical

Radical

◆

A Memoir
of
Wars, Communists & Work

Mel Fiske

Writer's Showcase
San Jose New York Lincoln Shanghai

Radical
A Memoir
of
Wars, Communists & Work

Writer's Showcase
an imprint of iUniverse, Inc.

For information address:
iUniverse, Inc.
5220 S. 16th St., Suite 200
Lincoln, NE 68512
www.iuniverse.com

ISBN: 0-595-24001-1

Printed in the United States of America

For Diana,
especially

and

my children
Michael
Daniel
Jessica
Andrew

and
my brother
Mort

The notion that a radical is one who hates his country is naïve and usually idiotic. He is, more likely, one who likes his country more than the rest of us, and is thus more disturbed than the rest of us when he sees it debauched. He is not a bad citizen turning to crime; he is a good citizen driven to despair.

—H.L. Mencken

Contents

PROLOGUE 1

CHAPTER 1   FAMILY 3

CHAPTER 2   YESHIVA BOY 23

CHAPTER 3   FARMER JOE 29

CHAPTER 4   BROTHERS. 39

CHAPTER 5   THE ARGONAUTS 59

CHAPTER 6   DIXIE LOU 65

CHAPTER 7   ON THE ROAD 79

CHAPTER 8   WARS. 89

CHAPTER 9   OAK RIDGE 107

CHAPTER 10   BEAD BOY 129

CHAPTER 11   ROUNDHOUSE. 143

CHAPTER 12   COILING PIT 155

CHAPTER 13   CORRESPONDENT. 175

CHAPTER 14   NEW YORK CENTRAL 181

CHAPTER 15   ALEC 207

EPILOGUE 219

ACKNOWLEDGMENTS

I could become effusive about the patience,
persistence and perspicacity of my editor,
Jerry Fleming, but I will not. All I will say
is that he is the best editor I, or any writer, ever had.

My thanks to Josephine Carson who started me off.

And to Leslie Kaufman for her skill in fashioning the cover.

My thanks to Charles E. Glover of the Palm Beach Post-Cox News Service,
who wrote the story quoted in italics throughout Chapter 8.

PROLOGUE

I wrote this for my children—to give them a sense of what I went through while growing up, of not only the momentous trials that shaped my life, but of important historical events that shaped our country.

While my kids figuratively are seated at my feet, listening to my stories, others can—and are invited to—lend an ear. The story-teller certainly won't mind. It's part of an old tradition.

There's something to commend memoirs to everyone. For the memoirist, it's a chance to review a life: the good and bad, the forgettable and unforgotten, the stupid mistakes and the rare wisdom. For the reader, it's a glimpse under the rock: lift it and see a new world.

In my case, it's a world of radicalism, the youthful exuberance of thinking it possible to change systems and beliefs. It grew out of resistance to unreasonable authority, a resistance that led me into many collisions with greater authority.

I could have accepted this authority—as many people have done and are doing today—but I wouldn't have turned out as I did. I didn't like to be cowed. I resisted, and was beaten and defeated many times.

I was called a radical, a Red, a Commie, a traitor, a terrorist. That's why this book is called Radical. I want my children and others to know that's nothing to be ashamed of, but something to be proud of.

1

FAMILY

I sat on a chair in a dark hallway, hearing the click of heels on the wooden floor as people ran back and forth between bedroom and kitchen and bathroom. Aunt Becky patted me on the head each time she passed. I sat quietly, my short legs dangling over the echoing floor.

There was a man in the bedroom with my mother, a man I'd never seen. He poked his head out the bedroom doorway from time to time to ask something of Becky and another woman, another stranger. The sleeves of his white shirt were rolled up and he had a towel draped over his shoulder.

I could hear muffled cries coming from the bedroom. I squirmed fearfully each time I heard them. My aunt, keeping an eye on me and on the bedroom door, stooped beside my chair to comfort me with a hug.

"Good boy, you're a good little boy," she murmured as she put an arm over my shoulders. I liked her hold on me. I felt secure, safe, and wanted.

She gripped my shoulders more tightly when a sharp cry came from the bedroom—then another, a high, choking wail, spasmodic and gurgling. I looked at my aunt questioningly. She gave my shoulder another squeeze and stood up. "Don't move," she said. "Be a good boy and stay here." She stepped across the narrow hallway to the bedroom, closing the door behind her. I sat rigidly, waiting.

Aunt Becky was my mother's sister-in-law, a few years older, and very pretty. Her daughter, Dotty, was my age. I didn't know where Dotty was that hot afternoon in July, but I wished she were there with me so we could play together. I wished I dared get off the chair to get my teddy bear. I wished my father would come home and let me sit on his knee.

The bedroom door opened again and the man appeared, rolling down his sleeves and putting on the dark suit jacket he held. He took a large watch out of his vest pocket, glanced at it fleetingly, looked down at me, and patted my head. He held the watch to my ear. I listened to the steady, comforting ticks, wondering again who he was. He put the watch back in his vest pocket and turned to my aunt emerging from the bedroom. She carried a small bundle wrapped in a blanket. He said something to her. She nodded and walked him to the door that led down the six flights of the tenement building to the world—the Bronx.

Aunt Becky took my hand, and still holding her bundle, led me into the kitchen. She sat down, held the bundle up, peeled away a layer of blanket so that I could get a better look, and said:

"This is your new brother." I stared in disbelief. Of all the strange events of the day, this was the strangest. How did *he* get here? Did that man bring him? The lady? What was a *brother*? A new toy? I stared at the red, wrinkled face, eyes pinched closed, lips twitching. The bundle squirmed and wailed that thin gurgling cry I'd heard earlier. She tucked the blanket over his head and went to the bedroom. I sat in the kitchen alone, hoping the screams wouldn't start again.

I WAS TWO YEARS and four months old when my brother was born that July 31, 1920. Except for that first day, I don't remember anything about Julie until he was two years old. What I do remember has been the stuff of nightmares.

We lived on the sixth floor of a walk-up tenement in a section of the Bronx that sixty years later became one of the worst slums in New York City, an area likened to bombed-out cities in World War II. I remember walking up and down the six flights several times a day with my mother. After my brother was born, I had to hold onto the railing and walk the steps myself, no longer carried up and down.

Though my mother was young and strong, it wasn't easy to hold a fidgeting baby with one hand, struggle to lift a carriage half-full of groceries with the other, up one flight of stairs, down a long dark hallway to another, then up four more flights, perhaps three times a day. The carriage couldn't be left on the ground floor or in the hallway; it would be stolen.

The apartment on the top floor was hot in the summer, a sweatbox, and my mother couldn't bear to be cooped up with two prickly, cranky children. She stuffed cookies, milk, sandwiches, toys and diapers in a bag and took her two boys to Tremont Park, the oasis in the neighborhood, once or twice a day. She pushed the carriage with Julie in it while I kept my hand near hers on the handle, through the crowd of children playing in the streets in front of the dingy, soot-smudged buildings—old even then.

In Tremont Park we crawled under iron railings to roll and play in the grass. My mother sat on a bench, one eye on her boys and the other on the *Jewish Daily Forward.*

Once Julie and I were playing catch with a small rubber ball when suddenly Julie picked up a rock big as his fist and flung it at me. I tried to catch it, but it struck me on the forehead. Blood spurted over my eyes, down my face and over my clothes. I cried in pain and fear. I'd never seen so much blood.

My mother jumped the fence, set me down on the ground, cradled me with one arm, and stemmed the blood with a diaper. She talked soothingly to me, dabbing my forehead, wiping my face. My brother stood impassively beside her, his brown eyes staring fixedly. He was two years old, and that is my second memory of him—and of my mother.

MY MOTHER ROSE CAME to this country from Baronovich, a railroad hub in Belarus, when she was seventeen—a small, pretty darkhaired woman, her hair fluffed over her right ear to hide a deep scar. A photograph of young unsmiling Rose, dressed in a flowing, tight-waisted, high-bosomed gown, reveals a woman coolly in control of herself and of her world.

A few years before the photograph was taken she'd been kicked in the head, above the right ear, by a bucking horse. She was unconscious for several days, close to death. The best doctors that her well-to-do father, a lumber merchant, could find were brought to the village to save the life of the baby in the family, his darling.

"Can I touch it?" I asked her one afternoon as we sat at the kitchen table. She lifted her hair above her ear. I touched the scar, red in the center, brown at the edges. I ran my finger along the rough depression and traced the horseshoe.

"Did it hurt bad?"

She shook her head. "I dunno. I was knocked out. I can't remember what happened. I was reaching out to touch the horse."

"Did a lot of blood come out?"

"Oh, yes. Lots of blood. But, see. It stopped. It got better."

At sixteen, she fell in love with a man her family thought beneath her station in life. Her father, a bearded orthodox Jew, stern, fervently religious, refused to let Rose see the man and arranged her passage to New York City, where her oldest sister Esther had gone a few years earlier. Years later, my mother told me that the long trip to the exciting new world helped erase her first romance from her mind.

"Was he like Poppa?" I asked.

"Oh, no. He was very handsome, but not as handsome as your father. He was a good singer and he played the mandolin and he loved to have a good time. But he wasn't in the yeshiva. And he didn't have a trade. He was the son of the butcher, the dirtiest man in Baronovich." She pulled me to her, gave me a hug and whispered, "Oh, Melvin, Melvin, he was such a nice, gentle boy. And he loved me. He loved me."

My mother's older sister Esther found a job for her in a garment factory on the Lower East Side, one of the few jobs available for young immigrants. Esther, an active member of the International Ladies Garment Workers Union, had just missed being one of the victims of the tragic Triangle Shirtwaist fire that had killed and burned hundreds of women workers. She'd worked at Triangle and quit the week before the fire to take a job in another factory.

A ten-hour work day in a sweatshop wasn't the kind of excitement my mother expected to find in America. She'd never worked in a factory, and, as the pampered daughter of a merchant, probably had never held a job. With Esther's help, Rose learned to operate a sewing machine, and in a few weeks was making her quota. After work, there was time for a few hours' talk and relaxation over the evening meal before sleep. She slept on a cot in Esther's small, dark tenement apartment in Manhattan's Lower East Side. In the morning, a hurried breakfast and a long walk through New York's wintry streets or across searing summer sidewalks took her back to work again. Only on Sundays did she have some fun.

At one of the Sunday dances organized regularly by the union for its young workers, my mother met Joe Fishkin, a handsome, mustachioed printer, also an immigrant from Russia. He'd not known a word of English, and yet now worked as a typesetter on the *New York Socialist Call*, an English-language newspaper. She was impressed. He was struck with her dark, flashing eyes, hourglass figure, no-nonsense attitude, and quickness of mind. They went together for more than a year, joining my father's friends, Sam and Anna Silver and Julius and Muriel Zabitz, on swimming trips at Coney Island, picnics in Central Park and the Bronx Zoo, and dances at the Workman's Circle Hall near Union Square. They were married in 1917, in time to keep Joe out of the World War I draft. They moved to the Bronx just before I was born, a year later.

AFTER SEVEN YEARS in the Tremont Avenue walk-up, we moved to Brooklyn. I don't know whether it was the oppressive heat in the apartment, the six flights up and down, or the stench of poverty in the decrepit tenement that led to the move. It could have been all three reasons, as well as the miscarriage my mother suffered—a miscarriage she told me about many years later.

Brooklyn was a comparative heaven, and Eighty-fourth Street a veritable garden. A tree stood in front of the two-story brick building where we rented the back ground-floor apartment, one of four in the building. Three steps up and a short hallway led to our cool, airy apartment. Our neighbors closed their doors quietly and their children didn't run through the halls screaming and crying.

We lived three subway stops from Coney Island, the end of the line, in an area of weed-choked fields and small farm plots tended by Italian families. Across the street from our apartment building was the cement foundation of an aborted building. It made a great playground and served as fortress, battleship, mountain and refuge.

On hot summer weekends my father would take my hand, my mother would take Julie's, and we'd walk to the subway station four blocks from our home for an outing to Coney Island. The fare was five cents each for them; my brother and I slipped under the turnstile. My father carried a bag with sandwiches and towels. We wore our bathing suits under our shirts and knickers. We pushed our way into the subway car full of people.

We couldn't afford the fifty-cents per person admission to Luna Park or to Albee's, where you could ride on all the carousels, wooden horse steeplechases, loop-the-loops, walk through fun houses with their distorting mirrors, or float on boats through dark tunnels. We'd stop briefly on our way to the beach and stare longingly through the fence at the shrieking boys and girls clinging to the necks of wooden horses sliding down the greased tracks of the steeplechase ringing the park.

Some days it wasn't easy finding an unoccupied spot on the beach among the million or so people who came for relief from New York's scorching heat. The best spots, near the water, were already taken when we came; we had to settle for a place near the boardwalk. That meant we'd burn our feet as we scurried through the sand to the ocean. The water cooled our feet, but we had to wade carefully for a dozen yards near the shore, parting the garbage pushed shoreward by the waves, before we could swim in open water. After a few hours, when we were ready to go home, Julie and I would go to a dark area under the boardwalk, thread our way among couples under blankets, peel off our suits, and put on dry clothes.

Sometimes on the way home, as we pushed through the crowds at the station, my father would give us each a nickel. The station was like a carnival with souvenir hawkers, candy shops, shooting galleries, baseball-throwing at targets of stacked bottles, bells clanging atop poles marked to indicate the strength of the blows of hammer-wielding strongmen. Julie would buy a fluffy spun-sugar cone, I'd have an ice cream, and we'd trade licks as we rode the subway to our Bay Parkway stop.

WE WERE LIVING in that apartment in 1929, when Wall Street crashed. I didn't know Wall Street from any other street nor the stock market from any other market, but I remember reading the headlines and I remember the man next door.

He knocked on our door one morning several months after the October crash. Thin, dressed in a rumpled grey suit that looked slept in, he held a long box as he greeted my mother.

"Scuse me, Missus," he stammered. "I wonder if you could help me out. I'm selling these," he opened the box with his free hand and thrust it at her. It held ties—men's ties. "Maybe you can buy one for your husband." She stared at the ties for a long moment, and then at him.

"How much?" she asked. One dollar, he said. She hesitated for another moment. A dollar was a lot of money. Even I knew that it was a lot of money; it would pay for twenty ice-cream cones. The box shook as his hand trembled.

"Wait," my mother said, and went to her bedroom. She returned with a dollar bill, rummaged through the stock of ties, selected one, and handed him the money.

"Thanks, thanks," he stammered effusively. "You're my first customer. Thanks."

My mother shut the door when he turned away, held the tie in front of her and shook her head. I asked her why she bought the tie if she didn't like it.

"Poor man. He worked on Wall Street and lost his job. He's trying to make a living. I'm just helping him out."

Weeks later, on my way home from a Saturday matinee at the Benson Theater, I saw our neighbor peddling his ties near the subway station. He looked hungry and angry.

My mother suspected him or his wife of arising—just after the milkman delivered two bottles of milk to our door every day—to skim the two inches of cream off the top and substitute water. She got up early one morning and opened the door when she heard someone rustling about in the hallway. It was our neighbor, barefoot, in his pajamas. My mother didn't say anything—just looked at him. He put the bottle of milk in his hand down on the tiled floor and backed off a few steps, then turned into his doorway. He didn't touch the milk again. He and his wife and their daughter moved away a few weeks later.

We moved, too, sometime after that, to a roomier second-floor apartment in a new building across the street from a farm on West Eleventh Street. My mother bought fresh vegetables from the Italian family who ran the farm; Julie and I watched their young sons feed the chickens, hogs and horses. One morning a moving van and another long truck came to the farm to empty the house and carry off crates of animals and tools. Then a gang of men tore down the house, the corral and pens. For months, I kept an eye on the construction of Seth Low Junior High School and park on the farmland. Years later, when I graduated to the seventh grade, I attended the school.

Two-story buildings, two apartments on each floor, lined the quiet streets of Bensonhurst. For excitement, my brother and I and our friends played stoop ball, a game in which a tennis ball, thrown against the steps of our building, had to be caught before bouncing.

We loved to go shopping on Bay Parkway with my mother: the dairy store with its great tubs of butter, salted and unsalted, displayed behind frosty glass doors, where pot cheese hung in cheesecloth sacks and large rounds of cheese rested on the marble counter; or the delicatessen, its barrels as tall as Julie, its aroma of pickles and brine and herring, its long salamis hanging from hooks behind the counter; or the butcher's, where my mother would select a live chicken and we'd watch the bearded *sochet* mumble a few Hebrew words before slitting its throat, and for a few extra cents pluck it clean. My mother would distribute her purchases and we'd carry them uncomplainingly as we made the rounds. We always got a little treat as we headed home—a penny jawbreaker or some sugar candy.

I WAS A SHY, SKINNY KID who would much rather read books like *Tom Swift and His House on Wheels* than play stoop ball with my brother or other children. Julie would play in the street until dark, and my mother would often have to drag him home to supper. My mother worried about my timidity and reticence. She encouraged me to join a Boy Scout troop and even took me to Macy's to buy a uniform.

One Saturday morning I met a scoutmaster and other members of the troop at the Bay Parkway subway station for a hike along the Palisades in New Jersey. We crowded into one subway car and transferred at Times Square to another train that would take us to the Dyckman Street ferry. I stood at the bow—my first boat ride—as the ferry plowed across the Hudson River. We hiked up a hill to an overlook, then along a trail through heavy woods draped in autumnal yellow and orange. We sang as we walked. It was the hit of the time: *There's a rainbow around the corner....*

At a clearing we made camp, as the scoutmaster called it. We collected twigs, and then rocks to enclose small fires. Some of the older and more experienced scouts fried bacon in pans and made delicious sandwiches: bacon slices between thin chocolate bars. I'd carried sandwiches made by my mother and traded them for these delicacies.

Then we took tests for merit badges. I flunked my fire-making test by using six matches instead of the required two.

Three days later I came down with a raging fever, diagnosed by the doctor as scarlet fever. I didn't leave the house for six months, and emerged on a spring day when new green leaves were sprouting from the young trees on our street. I never went on another hike with the Scouts.

Scarlet fever was a very serious illness in those days before antibiotics. My mother hurriedly sent Julie off to stay with Aunt Becky, who lived far out on Long Island. A health department worker tacked a notice on our door: **Quarantined—Contagious Disease**. I remember being in bed for a long time, reading dozens of books my mother borrowed from friends, making mechanical models with an erector set sent me as a gift, and playing Parcheesi and card games with my mother most afternoons. No one came to the apartment except my father, but I hardly saw him. He usually came home late at night, when I was asleep.

Sometimes I'd wake up and hear my father talking in Yiddish to my mother in the kitchen adjoining my bedroom, his voice high-pitched and agitated. "I don't know what to do, Rose. I work hard and at the end of the week there's nothing. I can't keep this up much longer."

"Joe, you've got to keep going somehow," she said soothingly. "You've got something of your own. No matter how hard it is, it's better than working for someone else. Better than being without a job."

"But Rose," he said, his voice rising. "I didn't even make enough to pay the rent next month. How can I keep going? With what?"

"Let me ask my brother again. I'll try to get enough for a few months. Now, come to bed. You're tired. I'm tired." The tea cups would clink as she washed them in the sink. The kitchen light would go out and I'd fall asleep again.

I remember overhearing many such discussions for the next few years as my father toughed it out with his printing business, which he named Melvin Press. He knew a great deal about printing but had no business experience. My mother, the daughter of a successful lumber merchant, had absorbed her father's business skills. She supplied the knowledge my father lacked and advised my father to keep knocking on the doors of the big companies. "They're the ones who always need printing," I remember her saying. "Don't waste your time on the small companies. They don't last long." With $300 borrowed from Uncle Alex, my father kept Melvin Press going and continued knocking on big doors. His persistence paid off, and he began printing accounting forms for Fox Films, the giant movie company.

"See, Joe, I told you," my mother said gleefully. "Now, when you get to know the purchasing agents a little more, you'll do better."

THE HOUSE WAS QUIET one Sunday morning, just a few days before the Contagious Disease sign was removed from our door. I awoke early and went to the bathroom. Through the thin wall I heard a strange noise, as if someone were jumping up and down in bed. I flushed the toilet. The noise stopped. I went into the living room. Nothing different there. I glanced through the thin gauzy curtain on the door separating my mother and father's bedroom from the living room. My father emerged from his bed without his pajama pants on. I saw his penis dangling as he stepped into his pajamas. I'd seen penises before—mine, Julie's, but I had no idea that one could be so huge. I left the living room, crept into my bed and pretended to sleep again.

Many months later, my father took me and my brother to Bensonhurst Maternity Hospital, a small one-story brick building at the intersection of Bay Parkway and Kings Highway.

"What's she doing in the hospital?" Julie asked. "Is Momma sick?"

"No. She had a baby. A little boy."

Neither of us had had any foreknowledge of the event. We hadn't been told a baby was coming. We weren't even aware of how babies came. I'd noticed that my mother was getting bigger and heavier, but most of the women I saw in the neighborhood were big and heavy. At Bensonhurst Maternity Hospital I put two and two together. I saw women teetering in the hallways with extended bellies, just as my mother had looked the week before.

It took me a while longer to figure out the relationship between a huge penis and a swollen belly.

"MELVIN. DO ME A FAVOR, PLEASE, and give the baby his bottle," my mother would say when I came into the apartment, put my school books away, and changed from new knickers to ones that had given way at the knees. "I have to take a nap. I just can't keep my eyes open."

With the warm bottle in one hand, and my baby brother Harold in the crook of the other arm, I went downstairs, where the carriage was parked in the hallway. I pushed the carriage down the three steps of the stoop, tucked the baby in with his bottle and stood guard, watching Julie and the other boys on the block playing stickball in the street. "You have to watch the baby," my mother told me. "You're the oldest. I can't trust Julie. He won't sit still for five minutes. You be my helper." I adjusted the baby's bottle when he lost his grip on it, and with one hand rocked him gently when he squirmed. I turned pages of my book with the other hand. I'd discovered the library, and such treasures as the *Tale of Two Cities* and *Two Years before the Mast*. Who needed stickball?

This was when I found journalism. I began reading the books and stories of newspapermen of the time: Vincent Sheean, John Gunther, Meyer Berger, Edgar Snow, Agnes Smedley. What a great life it would be, I thought, to be a roving foreign correspondent, or even a reporter on a city newspaper, to visit exciting places, to write vividly about events, to make other people feel they were there, seeing what I saw, feeling what I felt. I began writing for the junior high school monthly newspaper and can still remember my thrill when I saw my byline on a little front-page story in the paper. I was twelve. I'd written the story with the help of a dictionary because my English was tinged with the Yiddish spoken at home.

WHEN THE COLD, HARD WINTER gave way to sunny days in mid-February, my father carried Harold to the 1925 model Buick he bought for $50 in 1931. Julie and I trailed him down the stairs, lugging heavy suitcases my mother had packed. We were to stay with Aunt Becky on Long Island, and my mother made sure we had enough clothes to carry us through any emergency until she returned from Bensonshurst Maternity Hospital.

"Be a good boy and take good care of Harold," she whispered as I approached her from the side to kiss her on the cheek. I was afraid to hug her. A hug, I thought, might squeeze the baby out of her. I now knew a great deal more about such things.

My father drove with single-minded attention along busy Sunrise Parkway, a two-lane road that appeared to be made of corrugated concrete. The car, with its thin tires on large wooden-spoked wheels, shook and bounced. All his strength was required to hold it steady. He sat, tight-lipped, staring ahead at the road.

But he erupted when Julie and I, wrestling in the back seat, accidentally kicked Harold, who cried out in pain. My father took his eyes off the road for a second, jerked his head around, and roared: "Enough already. *Sha.* If I have to stop this car I'll give it to both of you. Now *sha.*" Julie and I knew that his anger boiled over at the slightest provocation, and that it often meant beatings with fist and strop. We all rode in oppressive silence as the windows of the car steamed over and our overcoats began smelling of wet wool.

At Aunt Becky's three-story Victorian house in Patchouge, my father unloaded us and our suitcases onto the big back porch. He waved to my aunt and then backed out of the driveway to return to Brooklyn. "Don't fight. Be good boys," he yelled, leaning out of the window as he turned into the street.

Two days later, he called. "It's another boy," he told Aunt Becky. I was standing beside her, with my cousin Dotty.

"Oh, Rose must be very disappointed," Becky said to my father. "She wanted a girl." I didn't hear what my father said. But my aunt whispered to us: "He's a beautiful baby."

We returned to the hospital on the day Morton was circumcised. In a small room off the lobby, a short, dark-bearded rabbi held the baby's kicking legs with one hand, and with a knife in the other nicked off some of the baby's penis. Mort screamed in pain and then whimpered for a few minutes. How can a rabbi hurt a baby? I wondered. Maybe he's making a boy into a girl, I thought. I looked around the room crowded with my mother's and father's friends and relatives. How can they be so happy when a baby is being hurt?

But if genes, chromosomes and the accidents of nature or a rabbi did not supply my mother with a daughter, she would *will* herself one. She dressed my brother Mort in pink. While he was asleep, baby-lovers would peek into the carriage, see his pink bonnet and coverlet, and exclaim "Oh, what a beautiful little girl." My mother beamed.

As Mort began crawling and standing, my mother attired him in pink dresses and pink rubber panties over his diapers. I was often pressed into service by my mother to tend him. I became adept at preparing his bottles of milk and juice, feeding him, and changing his diapers. I could see that he still had his penis. He was no girl.

The dresses were discarded in favor of overalls, but the hair—long, flowing blonde curls down to his shoulders—wasn't cut until he was five years old. On his birthday, after a little party, my father and my mother's brother Uncle Alex took Mort for a walk to a barber. The curls were shorn and trampled beneath the barber's feet.

My mother screamed in anguish at her brother when he returned, prodding Mort before him: "You've taken my baby girl…my little girl. Why did you do it? Who gave you the right to do it?" she sobbed. She glared angrily at Uncle Alex. To my father, hanging back, trying to make himself invisible, she cried: "How could you let him do it, Joe? How could you?"

"He's a boy. He's got to be raised like a boy, not a girl," my uncle retorted defensively.

Mort stood between them, looking from one to the other, bewildered. "I'm a boy, Mama," he said plaintively.

She sagged. Her head dropped forward. Her shoulders drooped. She turned and shuffled to the bathroom and locked herself in.

WE WERE LIVING in a ground floor apartment of a two-story building on Seventy-fifth Street, which was lined on both sides with identical brick duplexes, some with iron fences, others with low brick walls around small gardens. I was a student at New Utrecht High School, a six-story factory-like building two miles away.

The school was famous for the size of its student body—ten thousand, and for its track teams, which had won ten city championships in a row. I wanted to be on this team of champions, and since I was neither a fast runner nor a graceful high-jumper, I worked at becoming a long distance runner. Every morning, instead of taking the bus, I jogged along the Bensonhurst streets to school. My wind, stamina and stride improved as I ran imaginary races all winter.

In the spring, when tryouts for the team were called, I lined up nervously on the oval quarter-mile dirt track behind the school with a group of twenty other fifteen-year-olds. Tall and bony, I towered over my schoolmates. The young coach, Sol Furth, an Olympic broad-jumper, beckoned to me. "Let's see you jump over that." He pointed to a low hurdle upright on the track. "Lead with your left foot," he ordered.

I backed up a few yards, ran forward with short strides in my heavy, high-topped sneakers and sailed over the hurdle with my right foot. My left foot caught on the top wooden bar and I tumbled to the track. Furth looked on in disbelief, his tanned face frowning. "Why don't you work out with the cross-country team?" he said. He turned to the team manager, a senior student. "Give him a uniform—for trying."

Each afternoon after classes I put on my green and white running trunks and tank-top jersey and ran myself dizzy around the track with six other teammates. At the end of practice, I dressed hurriedly, rolled up my trunks and top with my books, and ran the two miles home, where I drank a couple of glasses of milk and watched my mother preparing dinner. She'd look up at me.

"You're getting so tall. Stop already and put on some weight," she'd say, and add wistfully: "I wish you could take some of mine." She looked down at her bosom, ballooning in her tight dress. "You're getting skinnier, I'm getting fatter."

I came home from school one afternoon to find my mother sitting at the kitchen table, her head in her hands. She looked up at me dispiritedly. Her eyes were red and a little swollen. Her hair, greying as her four boys grew in size and energy, was disheveled.

"Hey, Ma. What happened?" I asked.

She combed her fingers through her hair. "*Oi*, Melvin," she sighed. "Why is there so much *tsouris* in this world? And why do I have to get most of it?"

What kind of trouble is she talking about? I asked myself. I hadn't noticed any trouble.

"Whatdya mean, Ma?"

"*Oi*, Melvin. "She shook her head sadly. "Maybe I shouldn't talk to you about this." She looked up at me, her eyes brimming over. "But I don't have anyone to talk to."

"Why don't you talk to Pa?"

"That's the *tsouris*. I can't talk to him. He won't talk to me. He gets home late, when I'm in bed. He leaves very early, before I'm up. He treats me like a nothing. I'm a nothing. A nothing." She grabbed my arm. "Sit down, Melvin. Sit down." She pulled me into a chair beside her. "I don't know what to do. I tried sitting up, waiting for him to come home. But I fell asleep."

"Hey, Ma. Maybe he's working. Maybe he's got a big job in the shop."

"Working all the time? Never. He never did that before." She twitched slightly as if a cold shudder ran through her. Suddenly, angrily, she cried: "Just like Alex. Your Uncle Alex. *Oi.* My own brother. May he rot in hell." She sobbed. "*Oi. Oi*…Now your father…May they both rot in hell."

I didn't know what to say or do. What had Uncle Alex done? What had Pa done? I just sat next to her. With her right hand, she rubbed my arm resting on the kitchen table. She did it unconsciously, tenderly.

"Melvin, Melvin. If only we could take the boys and go someplace. Away. Anyplace." She gripped my arm and broke into sobs again. I sat stiffly, the chair suddenly hard and uncomfortable.

Her fingernails cut into my skin. I put my hand on hers and tried to peel her fingers back. I didn't know what else to do.

WEEKS LATER I NOTICED that my father was spending more time at home, arriving in the evening for dinner with the family, going out with my mother to Saturday night parties at the Sholem Aleichem Folk Shul and resuming his habit of sleeping late on Sundays. Life appeared to be back to normal.

My mother lost her disheveled, distracted look and went about her routine household duties humming Yiddish ditties as she made beds, picked up clothes, dusted and washed. Whatever had come between them had passed, I guessed.

But my father never hummed. And he rarely spoke to us. He would silently eat the meal served to him by my mother. When we finished dinner we boys would go to our bedrooms, Julie and I to do our school homework, Harold and Mort to play. My father would retire to the living room to read *The New York Times*. My mother washed the dishes. Except for the giggles from the bedroom of the two young ones, the house was silent.

One Friday night, before we left the table, my father announced: "I need one of you to work with me tomorrow."

"I can't come, Pop," I said quickly. "Tomorrow's the State Cross-Country Championship. Our team has a chance to win. I gotta be there."

He frowned. "Always some excuse lately. You haven't come to the shop for a long time."

"Every Saturday there's a meet, Pop. This one's in the Bronx, Van Cortlandt Park. Takes two hours to get there. I have to get up at 5:30."

"So you'll miss one time. Won't kill you."

"Oh, no," I protested. "The team needs me. I'm the number three man. I gotta be there."

He turned to Julie. "Okay. You come with me in the morning."

"I can't, Pop. I'm playing baseball in Prospect Park."

"That's not important. It's just another baseball game," my father said impatiently.

"It's as important as his," Julie snapped.

"His is the high school team. Yours is the little team at the park. You play with them every day."

"So, they need me, too."

"And I need you more," my father roared. "Enough. You're coming with me tomorrow. That's all."

"No. I'm not."

"Don't *no* me. I say yes—you're coming."

"No, I'm not. And you can't make me."

My father glared. It was the same look he'd always given me before grabbing his shaving strop to flail away at my back. Suddenly he pushed his chair away and at the same time lunged to grasp Julie's arm. Breathing heavily, as if at the end of a race, he pulled Julie to him. "I'll show you who's boss," he bellowed.

My brother, a muscular fourteen-year-old, twisted and writhed to extricate himself. "You can't make me, you can't make me," he cried shrilly. He dropped to the floor, pulled my father down with him, and struggled free. He ran down the short hallway into my parents' bedroom and banged the door shut. My father scrambled to his feet, ran to the closed door and pushed. My brother apparently had his back to the door. It held. My father hunched over, and like a fullback smashed into the door. It snapped open and Julie was knocked to the floor.

"Joe, Joe," my mother screamed. "Stop. Don't hurt him. He's only a boy, Joe." She held his arm, trying to restrain him as he stood over Julie, quivering on the floor. She glanced imploringly at the wall over the bed—at the large oval pictures of her mother, stern-faced with dark hair tied severely around her head, and her full-bearded father, wearing a black *yarmulke* over his sparse grey hair. My father shook her arm off, pushing her back into the hallway. He grabbed Julie by the arm again and pulled him to his feet, held the boy with his left hand, balled his right hand into a fist and pounded Julie's ear and cheek.

"I'll show you who's boss," he snarled with each blow. "I'll show you who's boss."

Julie, his face red with terror and anger, screamed "Let me go, you bastard. Let me go."

"Hah, calling me names now. That's what you think of your father, hah. I'll show you who's boss."

"Let him go, Joe! Let him go!" my mother cried. "Let him go, for God's sake!"

I pushed my mother away from the bedroom door and jumped on my father's back. Surprised, he jerked his shoulders, trying to shake me, then released his grip on Julie. I held my father tightly around the neck and pulled back. He twisted, turning from me.

Barrel-chested and powerful, he easily broke my hold. He whirled. I hit him on the eye with my fist. He stopped in shocked surprise and dropped his hands. I hit him again in the face. I don't think I hurt him. I couldn't hit him hard with my thin, puny arms. But he shook with anger and rage.

"You hit your father! How dare you hit your father! No son hits a father," he fumed.

"No father hurts a son," I shouted and flailed out again, striking him on the cheek. I was sobbing and choking with my own fury. All the years of absorbing his beatings—the fists, the razor strops, the belts—were erupting within me.

Julie stood in a corner, next to the mirrored vanity, rubbing his ear, looking apprehensively at my father, expecting another attack. My mother held her trembling hands to her head, cupping her ears. "*Oi, vey. Oi vey,*" she whispered faintly and sorrowfully to herself. My two little brothers huddled wide-eyed and silent against the hallway wall.

My father stared at me fixedly, his mouth half-open as he panted, his chest heaving, a hurt look in his eyes. "You hit your father," he muttered. "You hit your father." He stumbled out of the room, stepping around me.

He glared at my mother and pushed her roughly aside. My mother pushed back. "I'm not a little boy," she shrieked, tears streaming down her cheeks. "Don't you dare hit me. Never. Ever."

He stiffened and shook his head. His eyes filmed with tears as he walked away. He never hit us again.

2

YESHIVA BOY

I never learned about my father's father. Even in the brief conversations my father and I had about his boyhood in Russia, my grandfather was never mentioned.

All my father told me was that when he was thirteen years old he'd apprenticed to a printer and had left his house in Minsk to live with the printer and his family. He told me of sleeping on a straw pallet in a corner of the shop for five years, learning his trade from the printer who apparently was a taskmaster, then leaving to go into the Russian army as a draftee at eighteen. He was sent across Russia to Vladivostok in Siberia to serve guard duty on an army base. After a year of standing watches in the freezing cold, he was given a two-week pass to visit his family in Minsk, but he stayed on the train right through the city and on to Hamburg, Germany, where somehow he managed to arrange passage on a ship to New York.

A sepia photograph of my father and his close friend, my Uncle Sam, who married my father's sister, bore the stamp of a Bowery photographer and a date: 1915. My father is seated on a Victorian chair, his hand folded gracefully beside his cheek, my uncle standing awkwardly next to him, his hand gripping the back of the chair. Both are wearing fashionable suits and high rounded collars with large flowing cravats. You could see that they considered themselves men-about-town.

My father was twenty or twenty-one when that photo was taken. Uncle Sam was two or three years older. By the measurements of American society, they went on to have ordinary lives of little distinction; my father raised a family of four strapping sons in Brooklyn and built a good-sized printing business which he passed on to his sons; my uncle raised one son—my cousin Joseph—and ran a children's clothing store in New Haven. But both surpassed their wildest dreams and hopes for a future when they came to America.

ONE DAY IN 1980, on a visit to New York, I collided with my cousin Joe as he was entering a Manhattan hotel and I was leaving it. He was going in to call his wife, who expected him home for dinner, and I was on my way to a restaurant. He insisted that I have dinner with his family at his home.

Uncle Sam was there. It was the first time I'd seen him in twenty years. Now over ninety, he was still erect and energetic. His eyes glinted with humor, as if savoring a good joke. And his voice still boomed. It was the deepest voice I'd ever heard outside of the stage and concert hall. He sat back on the couch in his son's living room, fingering a cane held between his knees.

We'd last seen each other at my father's funeral, twenty years earlier. The thought saddened him. They'd been good friends when they were young and had remained good friends as brothers-in-law. "*Yussel* died too young," Uncle Sam said, using the diminutive of my father's name, a sign of love among the Russians—a love so great he named his son after my father.

I asked him about my father's family. "He never told you about your grandfather?" Uncle Sam asked. I shook my head.

"When I had sense enough to ask him about his family, he was dead," I replied.

"I met your grandfather Isaac when he was an old man already," my Uncle Sam began. "He was not yet fifty, but he was an old man. He'd been in the army for thirty years. How did that come about?" he asked, his deep voice rumbling as if he were asking a question around the Passover table.

"Your grandfather was twelve years old, a *Yeshiva bocher*. He was on his way to the school one day—he had his prayer shawl around his neck and his *yarmulke* and was carrying his books—when there's a clattering of horses hooves on the road, and all of a sudden the horses are all around him. He looks up and he sees Cossacks. The one with the fanciest uniform, the officer, says to him: 'Little yid, come here.' He pokes him here and there with a stick. 'Good, good,' he says. 'You'll do.'

"So a Cossack grabs Isaac and lifts him up on the saddle behind him," my uncle continued. "*Feh*. That's what they did in those days. They took Jewish boys into the army like that. Didn't ask anyone. Didn't have to get permission from the parents. The Cossacks were the law. They made their own law. They didn't ask. They took.

"Your grandfather was made a lackey. He cleaned up after the officers. He shined their shoes. He ran their errands. He washed their clothes. He groomed their horses. He cleaned their stables. He oiled their saddles. He made their beds. He cleaned up their *dreck*." My uncle's voice rumbled with anger.

"He did that for years. Years," he said, banging his cane down heavily for emphasis. "That's all he did. No school. No fun, except the drunken fun of soldiers on weekends. For years. He knew nothing, he learned nothing. Just the dirty work they made him do. And they spit on him. They hated the Jews.

"*Oi*, such a *shanda*…such a shame," he said sadly. "Hundreds of Jewish boys, maybe thousands, made into slaves." He lowered his head as if in prayer and was silent for a few moments.

"But it came to an end. Your grandfather was discharged after thirty years. After so long a time he was no good to the Cossacks. So there he was, forty-two years old. No trade. He knew how to take care of horses. He knew how to shine shoes. No one in Minsk needed a shoeshine boy, so Isaac got a horse and wagon and became a *droshky* driver, a teamster, a wagon driver," Uncle Sam said bitterly.

"If he made one or two rubles a day, he'd do well," Uncle Sam said. "That's maybe a half-a-dollar a day. As a single man he had a hard time making a living. But then he got married and had four children. *Yussel* was the only boy, the youngest. *Oi*, I tell you, Micchel, your grandfather had a hard life—a very hard life."

Uncle Sam meditated for a moment. "That's probably why he was such an angry man. A *meshuggeneh.* He'd come home at night with no money. Mad at the world. Mad at the people who wouldn't hire him, who didn't pay him what he asked. Always mad.

"He'd take it out on everyone around him. He'd beat his wife, his daughters, and Yussel. What else did he know? That's what they did in the army. That's what he knew. So that's what he did to his family. Many nights your father would run from his house and come to me crying, hurt.

"It was a hard life. Maybe that's why your grandfather wanted your father to learn a trade. Maybe that's why he found this printer and paid him fifty rubles to take your father in. I don't know where he got the fifty rubles. A small fortune in those days. But he got it."

Uncle Sam reached over and patted me on the arm. "Micchel," he said. "Your grandfather must have been a good man to help his son. He found him a trade. He paid the fifty rubles. Not many fathers did that. Mine never did."

He sighed heavily, took a deep, quick breath, and patted my arm again, as if to hold my attention. "For a long time, your father didn't think he wanted to be a printer. He wanted to run away from that shop. The printer was a terrible man. A *paskudnik.* Beat him all the time. He hit him every time he did something wrong. *Yussel* was so scared he couldn't do anything right. But he couldn't run away. Where would he go? Back home?

"If he went home, his father would beat him and send him back. After all, he paid fifty rubles. So Yussel stayed. He learned. He got to be a good printer. He was so good that when he came to New York he found a job right away. He didn't know a word of English, but his job was setting type. He'd read the words and pick out the type letters. So he learned English. Oh, he was a good printer. He made a good living."

Uncle Sam patted my arm again. "*Nu, Micchel,*" he said, "*that's* a story, ain't it?"

3

FARMER JOE

My father actually prospered during the Depression. His small printing plant in part of a loft in the old Tenderloin district of Manhattan had one employee, and printed accounting forms and advertising material for a motion picture company.

Pop would sometimes take me to that company's headquarters to deliver printing or to pick up new orders. He knew everyone in the purchasing department on one floor of a grey, six-story building extending a whole block on Manhattan's West Side. His special friends were the chief purchasing agent and two assistant agents who bought nothing but printing.

I helped Pop at the plant on weekends, and, over the years, graduated from making deliveries, sweeping floors and bundling paper scraps for recycling. Since I could type, he promoted me to do the billing. "It's the most important part of the business," he said. "If we don't bill, or make a mistake on a bill, we don't get paid." He explained his system to me, then watched while I calculated and typed the invoices.

I'd take each job ticket, total the costs, and add whatever percentage markup my father had indicated. Several of his customers were small firms; the markup on these accounts invariably was a fraction of the percentages indicated for the movie corporation.

At the end of each month I helped Pop go through the billings to the movie company. I'd read off the amount of each bill. I'd say *$240*. According to his system of cost-plus-markup, that meant $216 was the cost, $24 the markup. On a paper lined in three columns Pop would jot *$11* in one column, *$11* in another and *$2* in a third. Or if the total were $370, Pop would think a minute and jot down *$16, $16* and *$5* in the three columns. When we'd gone through the thirty or forty job tickets, he totaled the columns, wrote a check and asked me to go to the bank to cash it. I'd bring back a stack of tens and twenties. Pop would glance at his figures, count out three piles, place the money in plain envelopes, put on his hat and coat and take the subway uptown.

He didn't tell me what he was doing, but I put those percentages and the white envelopes together. He increased each bill by the percentage desired by the purchasing agent and his two assistants, plus a little more for *his* troubles. The agents ordered the printing at the inflated prices and were handed monthly cash kickbacks in the envelopes; my father got his printing jobs plus a little extra.

MY FATHER SPENT most of his life in cities, first Minsk and then New York, which he entered at Ellis Island when he was twenty. Twenty years later, he decided to buy a farm in New Jersey "to grow things."

He knew absolutely nothing about farming, but he had one friend, a chicken farmer, who advised him. I don't believe Pop took his advice, because he bought five acres of heavily-wooded land a few miles south of New Brunswick, close to a well-traveled highway. It was not farmland, nor could it be farmed without extensive tree cutting and clearing. Maybe he bought the land because it was a bargain. He paid cash for it in 1938, when money was tight.

In his brand-new four-door Chevrolet my father drove the family—my mother, my three brothers and I—to his farm on Church Lane, which indeed had a white-steepled church at the head of the road. A mile down the lane was the five acres of overgrown woodland. On the other side of the road was an authentic farm, run, we learned later, by an old Polish couple and their sons. The next neighbor was half a mile away. My father stopped the car and clambered down a gully and up a bank to look at his farm. I wish I knew what visions he had.

He was a tall, muscular man, with a massive chest that came from years of stacking bundles of heavy paper. He did everything there was to do in a printing plant—setting type, locking up forms, placing them on the press, running the press, cutting the paper, trimming the finished job, finally wrapping the package and making the delivery. Nothing was too menial for him, including cleaning the toilets. In the shop, he always wore his blue-striped printer's apron, tools sticking out of its pockets. It fit his hard body like a uniform. When he took the apron off and put on his double-breasted jacket, its pockets full of pads and pencils and packets of paper samples, he was transformed into a bulging, hulking man.

Finding out about the white envelopes and where they went didn't disturb me at the time. When I thought about it years later, I was troubled that my father was out and out bribing people for favors. I'd learned in my high school history classes that bribery was not countenanced in this country; maybe in other countries, but not in the U.S. But there were disturbing stories in the history books about bribe-givers and bribe-takers in the Civil War, and later in the Teapot Dome scandal. My father was now among the bribe-givers.

At the time, of course, he was thriving as a result of the bribery. He paid $762 cash for the new Chevy. I watched him count out the twenties at the car dealer and then sat proudly beside him as we drove up Kings Highway to our two-story brick row house in Bensonhurst to show the car to my excited brothers. He paid cash, too, for his five acres. Then he arranged with a master carpenter from the Old Country to build a house on the land.

Every weekend we'd drive to Church Lane to check on the progress of the house, which he and my mother intended to use mainly in the summer and on weekends. It was a neat, modest, rectangular clapboard structure built with care and craftsmanship. You entered the house from a screened-in front porch, through the square living room, and into a small hallway which served all the rooms. The hallway led to the bedroom my parents used, the bathroom, the bedroom in which we four boys bunked, and the kitchen. I had no knowledge of architecture or construction, but I appreciated the plain logic of the design.

My father knew Jake, the builder, only slightly before assigning him the job. But they became fast friends as the house went up. "I'll buy you a suit of clothes for doing a good job, Jake," I remember my father saying in Yiddish as he turned towards his car for the ride back to Brooklyn. He was true to his word. When the house was completed, he drove Jake to Crawford's and bought him the top-of-the-line suit at $18.75. Cash.

Jake was also paid in cash for his labor and materials. A reserved man with a wrinkled and weather-beaten face, he worked alone, at the same steady but seemingly unhurried pace. He'd begun the foundation at the start of spring. Four months later, the house was finished. It's standing to this day.

WE SPENT AN EXCITING but strenuous summer on Church Lane. Pop organized us into an army-like platoon in which we had jobs such as clearing the brush under the trees of the four acres remaining in the tract behind the house. He wanted a lawn in front, and the ground had to be raked several times, seeded, and watered. He thought it would be nice to have cantaloupes for breakfast, so we dug up many stumps to fashion a garden. He planted the cantaloupe seeds with much ceremony.

We worked hard, the four of us: I, the oldest, Julie, fourteen, eight-year-old Harold, and five-year-old Mort. We made a game of it, straddled the rakes, pretending we were horses, and it was fun. We also wanted to make Pop proud of us every evening, when he came home and inspected our work. He'd praise us but always point out some unraked spots, or brush that hadn't been pulled. Then we piled into the car for a ride to the quarry pit two miles from the house, where we'd swim in the deep, cool water. Mort had to use an old inner tube, and we'd keep an eye on him. The rest of us were strong swimmers, taught by Pop.

On weekends, my father did most of the heavy work of pulling stumps and chopping down deadwood. Single-minded, he was determined to finish as quickly as possible. Impatient with himself and with others, at those times he often showed a side we feared: his explosive temper.

The summer went quickly. We were all tanned and hard, and probably a couple of inches taller. We'd been fattened by the enormous servings of food my mother prepared from the fresh vegetables produced not on our farm but across the road at Skaritka's. This Polish family also had a few cows, so we drank fresh milk. Half-a-mile down the road another family raised flocks of chickens. Their two boys would run into the chicken coops and collect newly-hatched eggs for us.

Pop's farm managed to grow only a few cantaloupes and tomatoes, but you would have thought from his excitement that he'd harvested a major crop. Around the dinner table, before he cut into a tomato, he'd make a little speech: "See, out of a little seed came this beautiful tomato." He'd taste a slice. "Ummm. Delicious. Rose," he'd say to my mother, "Rose, taste this. You've never tasted anything so fine." His brown eyes sparkled as he looked around the table. "Such a good tomato. Boys, boys. You gotta taste it." Mornings, when there was a cantaloupe ripe enough to eat, he'd go through the same ritual. It became a family joke every time we had tomatoes or cantaloupes, even if they weren't from our farm plot.

The five acres—and we boys as well—were transformed by the summer work. The ground beneath the trees behind the house was leafless, like an unused brown carpet. The maple saplings in the woods grew straight and tall without the encroachment of weeds and brush. The lawn was green and shiny with dew from constant watering.

My father and mother decided to show it all off. They scheduled several weekend parties—one for relatives, another for friends in the Sholem Aleichem Folk Shul, and the third for the purchasing agents and their families.

My mother cooked for several days before the family came: Uncle Alex, her brother, a former bootlegger, and his wife, Becky, her bosom friend; Aunt Rose, my father's sister, and her husband Uncle Izzy, the Communist house painter; Cousin Al, the optometrist, and his wife Dora, a shy schoolteacher; another Cousin Al, a shoe wholesaler, and his wife Sylvia, a Park Avenue heiress to a textile fortune; Cousin Rose, a bony high-school teacher who looked like Eleanor Roosevelt, and her husband Tom, an Olympic high-diving champion who, it was said, had hit the water too often with his head.

My mother prepared cakes and pies with blueberries which we boys had picked near the quarry pit. She sliced and grated carrots from Skaritka's farm into a golden *tsimis*. She ordered chicken from the ranch down the road and boiled some of it for soup, broiling the rest for a side dish. She had a big pot of beef goulash simmering on the stove, next to a pot of boiling potatoes. The kitchen was like an oven, but she coolly and calmly orchestrated the feast without asking for help. She didn't want people getting in her way as she sliced, stirred, mixed, and whipped her concoctions together with extraordinary efficiency. She'd made cooking and housecleaning into an art form, though I knew from her many complaints that she resented being tied to house drudgery.

After hugs and kisses and hand-shaking and how-are-you's, my father would look at Uncle Alex and point to the kitchen. They'd inch away from the family and squat down before the cabinet under the sink. In rapid Yiddish, they'd weigh the merits of various bottles of liquor and agree on one. They'd fill two tumblers full of whiskey and lift and clink the glasses.

"*La Chaim.*" My father would take a deep sip and then sigh. My uncle would down the whiskey in one gulp, clap my father on the back and, in Yiddish, say: "*Yussel, Yussel.* Just what the doctor ordered." He'd hold his glass out for a refill. "All right. Now I'll beat you like you've never been beaten before."

Holding their glasses carefully, they threaded their way through the crowd of relatives to the porch where the checkerboard was already arranged and where they'd play fiercely, punctuating their moves with shouts: "Ah, hah. Now you devil. I gotcha. Let's see you block me now!"

"*Oy, vey*. He scares me. *Oy, vey*. What shall I do?"

"Oh, you sneak. You *momzer*. You *goniff*. You cheated me. I'll pay you back yet, you *farshikkereda schlemiel!*"

It was their vaudeville act, performed entirely for their own enjoyment. No one else was invited to participate, but if you wanted to enjoy, then, okay, enjoy as an audience. They would sit before the checkerboard for hours, getting up only for refills or to go to the bathroom. After playing together for years, they knew each other's moves, so their games were quick-jump, bang-bang-you're-dead outcomes. It didn't matter who won. What counted was losing themselves in the game and in each other.

My uncle had gone through a couple of quick fortunes as a bootlegger on Long Island. My father remembered going out on the Atlantic Ocean, beyond the three-mile limit, to help Uncle Alex smuggle in a boatload of liquor. It was scary business, he told me. He respected Uncle Alex for taking the risks. He was also thankful for the $300 loan Alex had made to him to maintain his printing shop. Alex, now broke and working as a bartender in a sleazy Third Avenue bar, sought out my father for whatever laughs and support he could get. They laughed together to drive away the realities of a poor existence.

When the officers and members of Sholem Aleichem Folk Shul Number Six came the next week, my mother produced another filling menu. But this crowd did more than eat and talk. On the horseshoe court the pins rang out constantly as shoes were flung from one stake to another. We'd built a large stone fire pit, surrounded with logs, in an open patch at the edge of our forest. There the believers in old Jewish folk tales and music sat on the logs around a blazing fire and heard shul members take turns reciting poetry or reading Sholem Aleichem stories. After a few glasses of wine, the singers began harmonizing their sad, haunting Jewish songs.

I went to sleep that night to their lullabies, but awoke when I heard a high, piercing tenor singing one of the raucous hits out of Harlem. The voice belonged to Isaac Cohen, a thin, bespectacled, unassuming man who looked like Mr. Milquetoast of the cartoons. He sang: "*Oy…Oy*…she was a low-down hoochie coocher…but Minnie had a heart as big as a whale…" Cohen always sang "Minnie the Moocher" after a little wine at *shul* parties. I knew then that my parents had hosted a good party.

MY MOTHER AND FATHER weren't as relaxed for their third event. This one was for business, and they warned us to be careful about what we said, not to boast about the farm, and to be on our best behavior.

My father wanted the lawn mowed, the flower beds raked, the drive-way washed down, and every leaf in the forest picked up. We worked for days until he was satisfied. On the morning the purchasing agents and their families were to arrive, we all pitched in to make the house as spotless as the forest. Then we helped Pop prepare his surprise.

He'd brought boxes of fruit hand-picked from a market. The apples, pears and plums all had stems still attached. Now we strung the fruit, with bits of cord, to the pines, firs, and sugar maples around the house. The two younger boys tied the fruit to the lower branches. We older boys tied the fruit to higher branches. My father got on a stepladder to reach even higher. We carefully put apples on one tree, making it an "apple tree," then plums on another. But my father was tying apples, pears and plums on the same branch.

"Pop," Julie yelled. "You can't do that. You gotta use one fruit only on one tree."

"Ah, what difference does it make," he said, looking down at us from his perch. "These guys are so stupid they think fruit grows in boxes."

While my mother finished up in the kitchen and my father greeted his guests, my brothers and I clustered together watching for the reaction of the purchasing agents when they spotted our fruit trees. My father led Mr. Beadman, the head agent, on a grand tour of the farm, and the two lesser agents and their wives, the Wollens and the Botskys, followed. They passed some of the fruit trees and glanced at them with idle interest. We pinched each other to keep from laughing as we tailed the entourage.

My father stopped at his garden of cantaloupes. He proudly pointed to the huge crop he'd grown: at least two dozen cantaloupes, a dozen watermelons, and some honeydew melons entwined in the vines. He stooped over and picked up a honeydew, which he handed to Mr. Beadman.

"Here, Bill. It's yours. Right out of my garden." Mr. Beadman took the melon in both hands, holding it away from his suit jacket, and looked at it distastefully. He thrust the melon into Mr. Botsky's hands, as if ridding himself of a hot potato. Mr. Botsky handed it quickly back to my father. "Let's get it later," he said. We ran off behind the line of cars to titter and giggle over our father's farce. We didn't dare laugh out loud and give it all away.

We watched the guests for hours, but they took no note of the strange fruit trees. All they were interested in was how much my father had paid for the land, the building of the house, how much the septic system cost and how expensive the couch and living room chairs were. I know now that they were adding all the sums up in their minds and thinking that they were responsible for my fathers' good fortune. So they looked at the place with proprietary interest and wished themselves in my father's shoes, for *he* could spend the gains of the percentage he added to the bills sent to their faceless corporation; they couldn't. They had to bank their bribe money in scattered bank accounts. They couldn't purchase new cars, invest in farm land, build country homes, or go away on expensive vacations. They couldn't draw their employers' attention to a burgeoning lifestyle. They had to live in small Bronx apartments and ride the subway and work until they reached retirement age, as if serving a prison term.

Mr. Beadman, a portly man with thinning grey hair and a blank, washed-out look, treated my father as if he were a lesser subject or a court jester. In a jeering tone, he said, "Joe, you're doing very well for a low-price printer. I must compliment you." He looked over at his two assistants. They grinned.

Mr. Wollen, a small, wiry man with a nose twisted from his days as a boxer, said, "Yeah, Joe, maybe you're going to have to raise your prices to pay for all this."

My father had a smile on his face and it froze. He looked over at my mother. She stared at him and shook her head imperceptibly.

Mr. Botsky laughed. It was more like a forced cough. "Cheh, cheh, cheh. You'd better not raise them any higher. Times are tough out there in the real world, Joe. Cheh, cheh, cheh."

My father stood up. His jaw worked angrily, and he swallowed a few times. Then he shrugged. "Let's not talk business. Come on. Let me show you I'm more than a printer. See my fruit trees. I want you to have some fruit to take home."

He led them to the maple tree festooned with apples. "Here—pick some," he urged. He waved his hand expansively to the other trees and added, "Help yourself."

Mr. Beadman plucked an apple from the branch. The stem was left dangling from the string. He pulled the string, looked at the other apples, and laughed.

"Hah, hah, hah, that's a good one, Joe. That's rich. Hah, hah, hah. Look at what he's done. He grows fruit with strings attached. Hah, hah, hah." He doubled over and slapped his knees, wheezing and shaking. "Oh, this takes the cake, Joe, this takes the cake."

Pop grinned, turned away, looked at us, and winked.

4

BROTHERS

My brother Julie and I grew up together: slept in the same room until I left at eighteen to go to college, played in the streets, wrestled each other like cubs, ate together, worked at jobs directed by Pop, helped each other learn to skate and ride a bike, played on the same sandlot baseball and football teams, traveled side by side on the subways to Coney Island or Manhattan, and on family outings sang songs and told stories.

Even though we didn't see each other for over thirty years, I thought of him often. Memories of him came up at the strangest moments. Once I was stretched out in a dentist's chair, and the time Julie and I went to a dentist in Bensonhurst floated into my consciousness.

I remembered the bare waiting room in the ground-floor apartment of the dentist, my mother's friend from Russia. Her office and living quarters were in one of the apartment buildings crowding 20th Avenue, a few blocks south of the West End subway. Thin, almost emaciated, she wore a short white coat. Her tightly-cut brown hair, just covering her ears, exposed a long, corded neck.

She was alone in the apartment when we came in, rose wearily from a chair next to the window, and embraced Julie.

"*Nu, boychick,*" she said in a deep, throaty voice. "You have toot-ache?" She gently drew Julie's hand away from his cheek. "Led me see." She peered in as Julie opened his mouth slowly.

"Tsk. Tsk," she clicked with her tongue. "*Oy.* Not good. Not good," she muttered, more to herself than us. "I will have to eggstract it." She turned briskly to me. "*Nu.* How's your mudder?"

"O-O-okay," I stammered, confused by her abrupt switch from mouth to mother.

She took Julie's hand and led him into her dental office, another barely-furnished room, with a tall ornate iron and leather chair, like that of a barber's, in the center under an overhanging light bulb. A cabinet with tools gleaming through glass doors stood in one corner, near the open window.

"*Nu*," she said, turning to me because I was older, ten to Julie's eight, "Vatt shell I do? Two dollars vit de pain killer or one dollar vit-out?"

I looked at Julie in the chair; he was holding his jaw, trying to keep from moaning.

"My mother only gave me one dollar." I took the bill out of my pocket and handed it to her.

She shook her head as she put the dollar in her coat pocket. "Hokay. Vatt can I do?" She shrugged and then turned energetically to Julie. "*Boychick*. Put your hands here and hold on. And you," she said over her shoulder, "vait in de udder room."

I sat in a hard chair near the door for what seemed like a long time, staring at the tan fly-specked wallpaper of the room, at the row of straight-backed chairs that once had been around a dining table, at the cracked and ridged linoleum simulating oak parquetry. And I listened.

"Ow. Owwww!" Julie cried shrilly.

"Hokay, *boychick*," my mother's friend said soothingly. "I know. It hurts. I vill take it out. Hold still."

"Owwwww."

It was a shiny day, the sun sparkling off the windows of the red-bricked apartment building across the street. Cars puttered by on the avenue, and in the distance, I could hear the rumble of the elevated West End subway on 86th Street.

Suddenly, there was a crack like a twig being snapped and a sharp, suppressed cry. "Ayyyyyy. Uuuuuu."

"Hokay, *boychick*. It's out. It's out. No more hurt."

I could hear the dentist moving about, the tinkle of her steel tools being collected and dropped on a tray, but not another cry from Julie. I wouldn't have been so brave, I thought.

After a few moments, she led Julie out. His jaw was clamped tightly around a wad of gauze that protruded like a cigarette butt. He wiped his eyes with his knuckles. then wiped his knuckles on his knickers to erase the tears. He looked so small. I reached around his shoulder to give him a hug. He shook my hand off and ran out the door.

We walked home slowly, Julie setting the pace. He shuffled, his hands jammed into pockets, his head down, his teeth clenched around the gauze.

I ALSO REMEMBERED the times Julie and I sat, bewildered and baffled, huddled on our beds, listening to our mother and father arguing. They screamed at each other in Russian because they didn't want us to know what they were saying.

Every once in a while they'd lapse into Yiddish, which we understood, and we'd hear words like *gesheft*, which meant they were yelling about the business, *gelt*—about money, and *shmattes*—about the clothes my mother had to wear.

Apparently business was not too good; money was scarce, and my mother was unhappy. My father felt her complaints an affront to his manhood, to his role as a provider and to his dignity. He lashed out at her with anger. His temper was explosive, as we both knew, and we looked at each other with alarm. Would he smash our mother with his fists as he did us? We wondered.

Mother's shrieks turned to sobs, the roars to guttural cries of *gevalt, gevalt*, then the door would slam shut with a crash that shook the house, and all we could hear were sobs. Julie and I would look at each other sadly—relieved, though, that he hadn't hit her.

It was soon after one of these recurring scenes that Julie came up with an idea of making some money: we'd open a nine-hole miniature golf course on a vacant lot on our block. We were living on West Eleventh Street at the time and had our pick of vacant lots. We chose one on a corner for maximum visibility.

We had no shovels or rakes, so we borrowed a broom and some knives from our kitchen and set about clearing the lot of trash accumulated over the years. Some stuff could be used: tin cans became cups at the end of each hole; old bicycle rims became obstacles on some of the holes; bedsprings became traps on other holes. We swept the entire lot clean and then roughed out the course with the knives, drawing each hole from tee to cup by scraping lines on the hard dusty ground.

Our Uncle Alex the bootlegger, the only one we knew who played golf, had given us two golf clubs and balls. He regularly went to the golf course to play with the district attorney and police chief. With his clubs we were in business.

We opened our course on a Sunday, charging one cent to play the nine holes—a bigger bargain than the ten cents regular miniature courses were asking. Soon we had a dozen boys and a few girls lined up to try their skill. Julie collected their money while they waited impatiently for the two players before them—and the clubs—to finish.

One of my friends, the son of the Russian general, stood in line for a minute but stepped out when Julie approached him and asked for his penny. The boy shook his head. "I not have any," he said in his slight Russian accent.

"You can't play," Julie told him.

I can't recall the boy's name, but I remember his hurt look as he turned away. I took Julie by the arm and whispered, "Let him play. He's a friend."

Julie pulled away from me. "No. Let him pay. Like everyone else."

We made twenty-six cents that day. We split it two ways. My mother didn't get any.

JULIE AND I GREW APART over the next ten years. I went to Ohio University, toured the country to write a book with four other college journalists, married a red-headed dancer, worked on newspapers in

West Virginia and Maryland, enlisted in the Marine Corps and spent three years on Pacific islands. I was mustered out in time to greet Julie in New York as the Queen Elizabeth brought him and ten thousand other Air Force and Army veterans home from Europe.

Julie staggered off the ship lugging a duffel bag that he slung into a truck waiting to take his group to Fort Hamilton for discharge. He'd seen us—my mother and father, Mort and me—waving from behind a barrier on the dock. He spoke to the truck driver and then ran to us. After hugs and handshakes, he reached into his pocket.

"Here, Mom," he said, handing her a watch. With its thin black band it looked more like a piece of jewelry than a timepiece.

"Here, Pop." He presented my father a large wristwatch with an elaborate gold band. He looked behind him for a moment, unzipped his field jacket, and peeled it off. On his arms, from wrist to shoulder, was a string of watches, twelve on each arm. He pulled them off. "Pop, hold these for me."

My father quickly began stuffing the watches into his jacket and overcoat pockets. He glanced around to see whether anyone noticed, but the hundreds of people on the dock and the lines of soldiers coming off the ship had other interests. My mother stood by quietly, looking at the son she hadn't seen in two years.

I studied him, too. I hadn't seen him in four years, and wondered what war had done to him. He seemed to be the self-assured Julie—still cocky, with the same cool, level stare. He was a little heavier and taller, a few inches shorter than I.

"Where'd you get all those watches?" I asked, as Julie gave the last of them to my father.

"Here'n there."

"You afraid to tell me?"

"It's no big deal. I got them trading with the Frogs."

"Trading?"

"Yeah. I'd give 'em cigarettes, cans of ham, powdered eggs. They'd give me a watch."

"Where did you get *that* stuff?"

"Quartermaster's."

"But you weren't in Quartermaster's."

"Didn't matter. I'd fix those guys up and they'd give me anything I wanted."

He had time to give Mom and Pop another hug as the truck driver honked his horn and inched slowly away. Julie scrambled up the tailgate and tumbled into the truck.

When he came home for good we drank Pop's liquor, swapped stories, and savored Mom's cooking. I could sense his hurt and disappointment as he told me about being drafted into the Air Corps, washing out first as a pilot, then as a navigator, then being assigned to aircraft maintenance.

"They had me gassing up planes and checking the oil. I was a gas station attendant." He serviced planes at Orly Field in Paris a few hours a day and took care of Parisian women (one in particular) and his black market activities the rest of the time.

He looked the same, but he'd changed. Something had cut away his old joyfulness and laughter.

We had one great party for our homecoming before I went off to a job in Washington. It was a wild, drunken night at my parents' home in Brooklyn. Friends and relatives came with cakes and delicacies and exotic liquors, and we tried to consume it all.

The house had large living and dining rooms on the first floor, three bedrooms on the second, and a finished basement that led to a small garden. The place teemed with people.

Most of the guests had come by subway, and we felt obligated to see them back to the subway, miles away, without mishap. Julie and I were enlisted to ferry the people in two cars—the family Chevy, and a borrowed Ford.

I was so drunk I couldn't see straight. I suspect Julie had difficulty, too. I made sure three people were in the back seat, two in the front with me, and I steered the Ford out 58th Street to 21st Avenue, up to

65th Street, over to Bay Parkway to the Sea Beach Line. Julie followed me. We caravaned in this fashion several times. When we kissed the last group of welcomers goodbye, he turned to me: "I'll race you home."

The cold night air had sobered me a bit. "Okay. But we can't start here. It's too busy. Let's go to 65th Street." He nodded.

We drove slowly to Bay Parkway and 65th Street and lined up at the corner. Julie raised his hand slowly and then dropped it. We jammed the accelerators, and the cars squealed off down the long street. He was ahead of me at the turn into 21st Avenue, and even though I pushed the accelerator to the floorboards, he kept his lead. We screeched to a skidding stop in front of the house. Julie jumped from the car, slamming the door behind him. "I beat you!" It was an exultant shout. It was as if he'd won a great Indianapolis Speedway race. "I beat you. I beat you!"

I DIDN'T SEE JULIE for more than a year, and then was invited to his wedding, a grand affair in the Waldorf-Astoria Hotel. I knew nothing about his bride except that she was a distant relative of my friend George, whose wife, Mildred, had told her mother about Julie. An elaborate matchmaking ritual was set in motion.

Mildred's mother went through lists of her relatives and found Gloria. First Gloria's mother had to approve. Mildred's mother arranged a meeting between Mrs. Johnson and Julie one afternoon. Mrs. Johnson liked what she saw: a tall, handsome businessman who talked about building his printing company and making lots of money. She saw security for her daughter. Security was important to Mrs. Johnson, a widow who knew what it was like to live without it.

She also respected single-minded business men and women. She was one herself. She'd taken over her husband's wholesale fish business and made a name for herself in a tough, man's world. She liked Julie's shrewd business attitude and determination. He was her kind of hard-driving man. They struck a deal.

Gloria, a pretty young woman with strikingly black eyes under a bobbed canopy of black hair, had no choice. She'd suffered a broken back in the accident that had killed her father, and had been in a cast in a Nebraska hospital for more than a year. The back never really healed, and she was to be in pain all her life. With her twisted back and swaying walk, she found in Julie more than she ever expected or hoped for.

At the wedding, dressed in a billowing white gown that cloaked her bent frame, she glowed. Her dark eyes, glittering with tears, bore through the mesh of her veil as she looked up trustingly at Julie standing beside her under the wedding canopy.

I was seated in the vast ballroom thinking vaguely of my two marriages: one by a Justice of the Peace in a small Kentucky town, the other before a few friends in a back yard in Virginia. My parents had not been present. Now they sat beside me and watched their second son intoning the marriage vows in Hebrew. I could feel their pleasure and pride, and had a twinge of self-reproach: I'd given them neither.

I had been infatuated with my two brides. Still was. As I watched this solemn ceremony, I couldn't help but notice that Julie didn't appear to be enamored of Gloria; he looked stiff and pained. I knew him well enough to see that he wasn't enjoying this. Why, then, was he getting married? More to the point, why was he getting married to Gloria? Had he found a soulmate or a business partner? He stood rigid and unmoving, towering over Gloria as the rabbi chanted the words that bound them together.

My brother Harold and Dolly, married just a few weeks before, were seated beside me. Dolly leaned over to Harold every few minutes to whisper her observations.

She leapt to her feet to cry *"L'Chaim!"* when the rabbi ordered Julie to stomp the wine glass out of which the new couple had sipped and pledged their life together.

"L'Chaim, L'Chaim," Dolly chimed, hugging Harold and then me.

"You know what Julie told me?" Harold asked as we shuffled into a line to kiss the bride and groom.

I shook my head. "I haven't talked to Julie yet."

Harold's voice dropped to a confidential whisper. Dolly pressed close to listen. "He told me Mrs. Johnson gave them a present of five thousand dollars."

"Five thousand dollars," Dolly said, awe and longing in her voice. "That's a fortune."

"Yep," Harold continued. "Five thousand dollars." He grinned and turned to Dolly. "What did we get? Five thousand laughs."

"We never can spend that," Dolly said ruefully.

I laughed with Harold.

JULIE CALLED ME ONE NIGHT in Washington. "I've got bad news." He paused and cleared his throat. "Harold died. He keeled over in the shop this morning. He died in the ambulance on the way to the hospital." His voice quavered. "They couldn't save him."

I listened in stunned silence. Harold: Only twenty-three years old. Just discharged from the Navy. Good health. Always with a joke, always with a laugh. The brother I'd helped raise. I loved him. He loved me. How could this happen?

"They think it was a cerebral hemorrhage. They don't know why it happened. And they don't know why it happened to someone his age."

Handsome Harold with your winning smile, why, why, I thought, did death pick you?

"The funeral's Saturday."

His life had just begun. He'd given part of it to his country and was picking up the pieces. Now there were no more pieces.

"Come home as soon as you can."

"I'll leave tonight. Keep the front door open." *Keep it open. Maybe it's a mistake and Harold will find the way home, too.*

Harold left a pregnant widow—the youngest widow in the history of Bensonhurst. Nineteen; a slim, flossy redhead. Years later, she told me how she'd learned of her husband's death.

She was surprised and suspicious when Julie appeared at her apartment that late afternoon in October. He'd called an hour or so before to ask her to be at home so that he could discuss a legal matter with her.

Why with me, she wondered, as she waited. Why not discuss legal matters with Harold at the plant, where the two work together?

Julie sat on the new plush couch in the living room of the apartment Harold and she had moved into a few months before. She was pleased with the appearance of the little room, with its classic Victorian-styled furniture. She'd spent weeks shopping, weighing the merits of each piece. She sat in her wing chair, peering at Julie.

He poked a finger into his collar. He loosened his tie.

"It's hot in here," he announced. "Let me open a window."

Dolly shrugged. "I'm comfortable."

He reached into a jacket pocket and withdrew a legal-sized paper. "My lawyers said it's important that you sign this."

"Why? What does it say?"

"It says you transfer all claims to the printing plant."

"I never had any claims."

"Okay. Then sign."

"But Harold has a claim. Why don't you get him to sign?"

Julie looked away. "No, this paper is for you."

"Why me?" Dolly looked quizzically at Julie. He came into focus. Sharp focus.

"Something has happened to Harold," she said softly, with sudden comprehension. "Something has happened," she repeated, her voice rising. "What! Tell me what happened to Harold."

"Just sign this paper," he grumbled. "Sign, right here. "

"Tell me. Tell me!" Dolly cried, her voice breaking. "What happened to Harold?"

"He died. This morning. At the cutter. He just fell down. Like somebody hit him with an axe."

Dolly stared dazedly at Julie. "He's dead?"

"Yeah. He's dead."

"He's gone?"

"Yeah. He's gone. He's no more." Tears streamed from his eyes. He turned away, sniffling. "He's gone," he whispered. He drew a handkerchief from a jacket pocket, wiped his eyes and nose, and thrust the legal paper in Dolly's hands. "Here. Sign."

Numbly, Dolly took the paper and pen, and scrawled *Adele Z. Fiske* on the dotted line.

She fingered the sheet of paper, crinkling it as if to ball it up. "Why did you wait so long to tell me? My own husband dies, I should be told right away."

Julie snatched the document from her hand. "I went down to the hospital in the ambulance. I couldn't call."

With a gasp of pain and sudden anger, Dolly screamed, "But you could call your lawyer. And you could go down to his office to get this dammed paper."

She turned, cradled her face in her arm and huddled against the side of the chair. She heard Julie get up, cross the room, ease open the apartment door and close it softly.

YEARS LATER, when my mother was on her death bed in a Manhattan hospital, I flew from Los Angeles to see her for what I knew would be the last time. I was invited to stay with Julie and Gloria in their rambling ranch house out on Long Island, an hour or so by train from New York City.

My mother had a brain tumor. She could neither talk nor move her hands, but we managed to converse when I found she could move her toes. I told her to move a toe once for *yes* and twice for *no*.

I sat beside her bed and rubbed her limp arm and told her stories about her two grandchildren, whom she'd seen a year earlier. She tried to smile at my descriptions of their antics, but the smile smeared her face into an ugly grimace. Even that was an effort, and she'd close her eyes and sink into herself, to find renewed strength. After a few moments her eyes blinked open and looked expectantly at me.

Tell me more, they said. *Talk to me some more. Tell me things you kept from me. Tell me why you left me, my first born*, her eyes pleaded.

"I love you, Ma." I can't remember having said that in all my years, nor do I remember anyone in our family—not even my father—saying it to her. Open expressions of love were to be found only in the movies she went to every week, not in our family.

Her eyes fluttered. I thought she was going to cry, but her tear ducts were paralyzed and she couldn't.

"It's all right, Ma." I kneaded her arm. "We all loved you, Ma. Even though we never said it."

Her eyes fluttered and remained shut for a moment. What was she thinking?

I sat and stroked her arm. Her face was in repose, and she looked like the younger, thinner Rose of my high school days, when I'd struggled to break away from her and home.

She opened her eyes. There was hurt and sorrow in them.

Oh, my first born, they said, *how could you know the pain I suffered in a family of five self-centered men to whom I gave my youth and energy and life? How could you know, you who fled my embrace, who broke my heart, who caused me untold anguish. And now you tell me that you love me, now as death strangles me. It comes too late. Too late. It cannot save me.*

And she shut her eyes firmly. I could see her eyes quivering under the lids. I had not been able to talk to her in life as I was growing up. She could not talk to me as life was being choked out of her.

JULIE'S HOUSE was in landscaped woods at the end of a dead-end lane. It had four bedrooms, one for Gloria and Julie and one each for the three children. There was a study with a long couch for guests.

I don't know how I made my way to the Long Island Railroad Station to meet Gloria, who drove me home in the old Rambler that had been my mother's. I was full of my mother's pain and agony, full of my regret and guilt.

Gloria made numerous trips to the kitchen to fill our plates, but I can't remember what was on them. I tried to tell Julie, as we sipped wine, how I'd felt when I sat with our mother.

He shrugged. "I know how she was," he said, dismissively. "After all, she lived here until a few weeks ago."

Julie and I sat in the study, in leather easy chairs, surrounded by colorful prints of English hunting scenes. He talked: about the tremendous growth of the printing plant after Pop died, all of it due to the new accounts he'd brought to the shop. And to the new equipment he'd bought to keep up with the new orders.

He talked: about his Long Island estate, which had increased in value three-fold since he purchased it. And the new lawn mower on which he perched every weekend to cut his acre of lawn.

He talked: about the new station wagon he'd ordered from the local Dodge dealer who'd neglected to honor one clause of an agreement. Minor though the clause was, Julie sued the dealer for breaking the agreement and gotten the wagon for only the down payment.

He talked: about the increased power he'd have over the printing plant now that all of my mother's shares would revert to him when her will was opened. He'd buy another four-color press and take the shop into the big-time.

He talked, leaning over me from his wing chair. I listened, stretched out on the couch. I heard him with one ear, sorted out my impressions about the hospital visit in another part of me, and tried to keep awake.

Not once did he ask me about my life in Los Angeles. About my wife. About my three children. About my work. About my thoughts.

I fell asleep as Julie droned on.

MY YOUNGEST BROTHER, Mort, his wife Perle and I visited my mother at the hospital before I left New York. We brought a bouquet of roses, her favorites, and set them on the dresser facing her bed.

Her eyes, without the horn-rimmed glasses she'd worn for years, were wide, straining to see everything, shifting from one face to another, to the roses, then back to us at the foot of the bed. She couldn't move her head.

I pulled back the sheet at the end of the bed to expose her toes. "Ma. Let's talk. Move your toe once for *yes* and twice for *no*. Okay?"

One toe moved as we all watched.

What do you ask a woman you've known all your life, who knows everything about you except your secrets and about whom you know everything, except her private self, her hidden thoughts? We have two parts to us, I thought, the public side and the private side. One for show, the other for torment.

I looked at Mort, stooping slightly as he fingered the bars of the bed, his hands twisting nervously. His wavy brown hair was brushed back in a pompadour, his face broad and square-jawed, my mother's male replica. No wonder her eyes always sparkled when she saw him.

Mort glanced down at Perle standing close to him, as if she sought protection. Blonde hair fluffed out above the collar of her tight-fitting dark grey suit. Even in high heels she was tiny, almost birdlike, next to Mort.

It took a lot of courage on Perle's part to visit the rejecting mother-in-law. She hadn't wanted to come, but Mort insisted. "You're my wife. She has to accept that."

Mort cleared his throat. "Would you say you had a good life, Ma?" he asked gently. I looked at him gratefully and then down at the toe.

My mother pulled down the curtain of her eyes briefly. Her toe wiggled slowly, once.

She shifted her gaze from one to the other as she waited for the next question.

"Were you happy with Pa?" I asked. It was a loaded question but I blurted it out before thinking. I remember the nights when she would talk to me about how uncaring my father was, how he mistreated her, and how she thought of taking her boys and running away from him.

Her toe moved, once.

Good. Time heals all, I thought. She thinks now of the few years before his death, when they traveled around the country like honeymooners.

Mort cleared his throat again. "Ma, would you give us and our marriage your blessing?" He threw an arm around Perle.

I wasn't watching her face—just her toe. There was an almost immediate reaction. The toe moved once.

Mort gripped Perle's shoulders. Tears began spilling down his cheeks.

I kept looking at the toe. I could have sworn there was another movement, a twitch, but Mort and Perle didn't see it.

MORT HAD BEEN WORKING with Julie at the printing plant for years, before and after the war. Julie was his mentor, and the two of them were to manage the shop together, now that Harold was dead and I wanted no part of it. It was their shop, and, after my father's death, my mother had made it known to everyone in the family that she was passing it on to the two of them.

So I was shocked when her will was opened, several weeks after her burial, to learn that she'd cut Mort out. She'd turned over all her shares in the printing plant to Julie.

Her grievance against Mort was deep. Mort had married Perle, an older woman with a child, against her advice and desire. Perle was vivacious, a self-made woman who'd climbed her way up the career ladder in a leading construction company. She wasn't the woman my mother had visualized for her son.

I don't know what woman would have satisfied my mother, but Perle didn't. I don't believe she was happy with any of the women her sons chose to marry.

Mort was baffled and angry. He retained Paul O'Dwyer, brother of the then-New York mayor, and contested the will.

O'Dwyer determined that my mother had changed her will while she was in Julie's care in his house, a month or so before I saw her in the hospital. A codicil had negated all previous stipulations to distribute the shares equally between her two sons.

Mort's lawyer charged Julie with fraud and undue and improper influence on a dying woman and asked the probate court to nullify the will.

During pretrial depositions, it was learned that Julie had taken my mother out of a hospital, installed her in one of his bedrooms, and hired professional nurses to care for her around the clock. The nurses also witnessed the typewritten codicil when it was signed, in mother's shaky hand. Soon after she signed, she was transported back to the hospital.

Mort's lawyer hired investigators to find the nurses, but they were not to be found.

I was informed about all this in long phone conversations with Mort, and I was disturbed but not surprised. I remembered Julie telling me about his plans for the printing plant now that he was getting all the shares. He knew then what the will would say. I agreed to testify in Mort's behalf about my mother's intentions and about Julie's statement to me.

But I didn't have to testify. Just before trial, the lawyers worked out an agreement giving Mort a sizable sum in return for Julie's clear title to the plant.

Mort explained later, "I wouldn't work with the bastard even if I was given my due share. How could I work with him? I thought it best to take the money and get the hell out."

The brotherhood was broken: Mort and I banished Julie; he excommunicated us.

ONE DAY IN THE SPRING OF 2000, Julie's daughter, Sandy, called to tell me that her father was on his deathbed. "Don't you think it's time for closure, time for healing?" she asked. I told her I'd thought so for the last few years, and had made several overtures to Julie. "Only to be rejected every time," I added.

"If he wants to see me, I'll come down, but he has to want to see me. I don't want to be rejected again," I said. Sandy called me the next day, and I caught the redeye to Miami that night. Mort met me at the airport and we drove to Julie's home in Naples. During the four-hour ride we talked about his misgivings over the meeting, and my need for it. "After all," I said, "I grew up with him. We did everything together. I have to see him once more before he dies."

Mort left me at the house, a ranch-type near the bay. Sandy and her brothers, Richard and Paul, greeted me at the door and led me to the living room, where Julie sat in an overstuffed arm chair. He rose firmly, but with some effort, and gripped me in a tight hug. He hung on for a minute or more, then dropped his arms and sat down heavily. He rubbed his eyes. They were teary, like mine.

His children and his wife Gloria sat on the couch, watching this reunion, this unfolding drama, anxious about its outcome. Gloria, black hair shining and styled, shook my hand, briefly taking her eyes from her husband. Julie was breathing heavily; his son, Richard, a homeopathic healer, came to his side and inserted plastic tubes into his fathers' nostrils. The tubes ran through the living room to oxygen tanks in another room. I sat beside my brother, sadly noting his protruding belly, his labored breathing, his shrunken frame, his rheumy eyes. Age, emphysema and cancer had caught up with him.

The oxygen revived him. He began recounting what seemed to be every business deal and business he'd been in, every move, every trip he'd ever taken, every painting—his walls were covered to the ceilings with paintings and drawings—and their painters, his fortune, his investments and the accolades he'd received in the local newspaper for operating a Naples supper club. "Sandy," he ordered at one point, "go get that editorial about me." He droned on, much the same way he had thirty or more years before. Stopping to adjust the oxygen tubes, he said: "Hey, I've been doin' all the talking." He smiled broadly and nodded to me, as if he were holding a door open, permitting me to enter. "Tell me about yourself."

I fumbled for words. Where would I start? Thirty years ago? Yesterday? "You may know," I began, "I started a magazine in Los Angeles about twenty years ago...."

"Oh, Los Angeles," he interrupted. "I was there seven years ago...Let's see...no, it was 1994...six years ago...Wasn't it, Gloria?...and I went to...which studio did we go to, Gloria?..." It was a blow-by-blow description of his week-long visit. I never got beyond a tentative introduction to my life. He never asked me about my wife, my children or my work. He hadn't changed much in thirty years.

I was his guest that evening at a birthday dinner for Gloria in the Ritz-Carlton Hotel. His sons placed him in a wheelchair and pushed him to the festive table. I sat next to him and matched him glass for glass as he lavishly poured the wine. He offhandedly made a caustic remark about Mort. I resented it, and said so. Our argument became heated and we glared at each other, just like the old competitive days. I glanced at Sandy and Richard and Paul and saw, in their faces, a plea to pull back from the brink. Sandy even kicked me under the table. It was Gloria's birthday party, after all. They'd never thought they'd be celebrating it with her, for she'd undergone major heart surgery and years of recovery. Her poor health had compelled Richard to study homeopathic medicine, and he'd nursed her to this milestone.

They were especially afraid that Julie would explode in anger; they told me so the next morning when we had breakfast together in the downtown hotel where Mort and I stayed. "He's a madman when he erupts," Richard explained. "He was close to it last night. I could tell. I've seen enough of it all my life."

They told me, over the long breakfast, of a side of my brother I'd never seen or imagined. He was unpredictable: a tyrant or a loving father; his word was law yet he was forgiving; when they were children he beat them at the slightest provocation, yet was generous to a fault. Richard remembered huddling on the roof, outside the window of his room, to escape. Sandy remembered spending many nights at a friend's. Paul remembered playing the fool to make him laugh and avoid his wrath. It was an outpouring of sorrow over their twisted, unloved lives, yet it was also a cleansing, a grasp for understanding—for renewal, for sanity.

They wanted to know from me and Mort—whom they'd seen only once or twice in their lives—why their father had been such a Jekyl and Hyde—angry, tyrannical, brutish one minute, and charming, secure, confident and considerate the next.

Just like my father, I said.

5

THE ARGONAUTS

I hitched onto the labor movement in an oblique way in May, 1939 when a cheerful, stocky young woman confronted me in the Newspaper Guild office in New York City's midtown.

I saw her peering at me as I fingered the sheaf of "Help Wanted" notices tacked to the bulletin board. Her curly hair fluffed out like Little Orphan Annie's; she was dressed in the uniform of the co-eds I knew in Ohio University—baby blue angora sweater, full skirt and low-heeled saddle shoes. I edged away, but she stepped in front of me.

"Can you drive a car?" she asked.

What a funny question. "Yeah…sure," I stammered. "Why?"

She looked up at me. "Well, we need someone to drive us around the country." She smiled disarmingly, cherubically. "Would you like to come with us?"

I looked down at her. "Go with you?…Around the country? Just like that? You're kidding me."

"No. I'm serious." She pursed her lips. "You're in journalism, right? Otherwise you wouldn't come to the newspaper union hall, right?" She grinned, pleased with her deductions. I nodded. She rushed ahead. "I've got three other students. We're going to the Newspaper Guild convention in San Francisco. I've got a car. We need a driver. Want to come?"

This girl didn't believe in wasting words. She stood planted before me. Her look challenged me.

My mind raced through my alternatives: take my chances on scrabbling up a newspaper job—of which there were few, as the bulletin board revealed; go back to my father's printing shop—work I'd hated ever since I was nine, when he pressed me into service; get any other menial job to make enough money for tuition, books and bus fare. Or grab this opportunity for a summer of adventure, seeing the country. From sea to shining sea.

"Hell," I said. "Why not? When do we start?"

That impetuous decision, made in the depths of The Great Depression, was one of the best in my life.

Her name was Lillian, editor of the student newspaper at Hunter College in midtown New York. She was the spark plug. She beguiled Joe, editor of the Brooklyn College newspaper, George, editor of the City College of New York paper, and her sister Helen, a writer and unemployed waitress, to drive cross-country to form a student chapter of the American Newspaper Guild. After the convention there'd be time to poke around corners of the country.

A determined and skillful organizer, Lillian arranged to borrow a brand-new Plymouth sedan for the trip, amassed a list of relatives, friends, and friends of friends around the country to drop in on for a night or two; she raised money for gas, food and incidental expenses, and interested a publisher in a book about the trip. Now that she'd found her driver, she set the departure date for July 15.

I had to come up with my share of expenses, $50—a huge sum then. I went through uncles and aunts, cousins and friends. Most were living hand-to-mouth and had to think twice before handing over a dollar or a fiver to a twenty-one-year old intending to throw their money to the winds in a wild joyride.

My entreaties brought $47. Lillian shrugged, took the money and handed it to George, our treasurer.

I also had to take a driving test. Lillian's father sat in the back seat as we picked up the Plymouth at a dealer's garage. Her father was a compact, muscular man who looked as if he spent lots of time outdoors. I watched him from the rear-view mirror. He said nothing, his lips pursed, looking critical. I drove him ever so carefully to his Brooklyn duplex, where he met Lillian. He nodded approval. "Good driver," he said. "You'll be safe." Lillian beamed, her judgment vindicated.

THE NEXT DAY WAS JULY 15. I drove the Plymouth, now sagging on its springs with this load of five well-fed youngsters and their suitcases, along tree-lined streets, over the Brooklyn Bridge, through clamoring Manhattan traffic and the Holland Tunnel under the Hudson River, to the wide-open spaces of New Jersey. We made our first stop at Lake Farrington, where my parents were spending the summer. My mother added to the overburdened car by thrusting boxes of sandwiches, cookies and cakes into our hands "so you won't go hungry."

When we took to the road again, I felt a soaring energy. The last parental tie had been cut; we were outside the confines of the Big City. The car was a rising balloon, floating over the road. The country, its mysteries, its histories, and its ribbons of road stretched before us. The look of the land, its vastness, the green rolling hills, the clean compact towns pleased me, like views of beautiful paintings. I held to the speed limit of 45 miles per hour on the two-lane highways, and felt exhilarated.

Bearing my right foot down on the stiff accelerator hour after hour was nothing compared to the contortions George, Helen and Joe had to endure in the back seat, crammed with excess clothing, books and food that wouldn't fit in the trunk. They fussed and fumed trying to find comfortable positions.

My seat was assured; I was the only one who could drive. Lillian, sitting beside me, organized us into a "city room," modeled after the editorial office of a big-city newspaper. Naturally, she sat in the front seat, akin to the slot in a city desk reserved for editors, and issued assignments to us when we came to a city, or stopped for gas, or pulled up beside tourist cabins for the night in those days before motels.

We all had notebooks, and on their pages we scribbled our impressions of the countryside, the comments of people we interviewed, and our own bright sayings. Lillian instructed us to talk to anyone and

everyone and observe as much as we could. Good training for reporters.

Helen, a taller, blonde version of her sister, was put in charge of
"food and lodging" because of her experience as a waitress and office
worker. Twenty-year-old George, with his recent degree in business
administration, was appointed the "finance department." Joe, at nineteen the youngest and still growing, was named "librarian" to keep
track of the clippings and notes we accumulated.

Our first long stopover was in a remote area of the Blue Ridge Sum-
mit in Pennsylvania. In a secluded house on a hill well off the highway,
we met Jay Franklin, a nationally-syndicated columnist. He was one of
the names in Lillian's book and we wanted to talk to him, Lillian said,
"to get a line on people and things to see."

(Many years later, I read a magazine article about Jay Franklin.
Under this pseudonym, and as a columnist, he traveled around the
country ferreting out information to help President Roosevelt develop
strategy on programs, to formulate policies, and even to get some dirt
on FDR's enemies. According to the article, he established an internal
spying network for the President. I'm not sure whether Lillian knew
this at the time, but I assume we became, wittingly or unwittingly, part
of that network.)

After the heady experience of interviewing a famous columnist, I felt
we'd come up a step from being mere college kids. Indeed, I considered
us serious journalists, probing for whatever truth existed in the country.

AT FORTY-FIVE MILES per hour, no faster because of the Plymouth's
overloaded springs, we emerged from the forested Pennsylvania mountains through grimy, smoky Pittsburgh, speeding past small industrial
cities in Ohio, staring at the shuttered factories on both sides of the
road. We stopped in Cleveland to interview striking auto workers pick-
eting the giant Fisher Body plant. Then we drove along Lake Erie,

through Toledo, Ohio and Gary, Indiana, to Chicago. Lillian checked her list and called a Newspaper Guild friend.

We met him at the Guild's strike headquarters, a former speakeasy and nightclub in Chicago's downtown financial district. We stayed a few days, longer than our schedule allowed, joining Hearst newspaper strikers on the picket line they'd been walking for eighteen months. Then we had to race to the coast to get to the convention in time.

We lightened the load on the springs by shipping a hundred pounds of baggage ahead. I drove many hours in daylight and many at night, through Missouri corn fields, through the flat, dusty Kansas lands, the mountains of Colorado, the Utah desert, and across scrubby Nevada to San Francisco, the "roller-coaster city."

I fell in love with that sparkling city. It became, for me, the most memorable place we visited in our 92-day coast-to-coast-and-back journey of 15,150 miles. After the convention, we trekked up to Seattle, down to Los Angeles, and around California's Central Valley for several weeks, then wound our way south through Texas and Louisiana for several more. We ran out of money in Texas and again in Tennessee. With the help of a few financial angels, we finally made our way back home via Washington, D.C.

The story of the adventure appeared in a book published a year later by Modern Age Books. Called *The Argonauts,* the book sold for $2.50 in hard-cover. We began writing it soon after October 15, when we returned to New York. On the windowed sun porch in Lillian and Helen's home each of us wrote two chapters, sharing the records in our notebooks. When we collated the ten chapters, the first draft established that "writing by committee" didn't work too well. Lillian took on the job of rewriting and polishing the book in one style and voice to the publisher's satisfaction. I'm sure it wasn't satisfying to him that only 650 copies of the book were sold.

To appease prevailing but unspoken anti-Semitism, the publisher asked us to Americanize our names. Lillian and Helen Rosovsky became Lillian and Helen Ross; George Weissman became George

Whitman; Joe Wershba stuck by Joe Wershba, and Mel Fishkin was renamed Mel Fiske.

WHAT I SAW AND HEARD as an "Argonaut" made me think intensely about our country and the future of its people. I no longer pondered dry statistics in a textbook. I saw with my own eyes a country in agony.

I saw the Hoovervilles, the tin and cardboard shacks on the dreary edges of cities, buried and forgotten cities within cities, where people withered away in rags, hunger and sickness.

I saw For Sale signs standing like rows of fences before countless homes on the streets of towns we rushed by.

I saw the Okies—the people of Oklahoma driven from their land by the great dust storms and depression of the '30's—in caravans of battered cars and trucks loaded with families and their possessions, wandering from field to field in California in search of any jobs.

As "Argonauts" we were searching for more than the Golden Fleece. We searched for answers to the questions we saw around us. We talked about the country's problems as our Plymouth rolled along the roads.

One night on the long drive from El Paso to San Antonio, Joe sat beside me. He'd been assigned to keep me awake, while Helen, Lillian and George slept in the back seat. I gripped the wheel, staring ahead at the narrow black highway as Joe talked. I wondered how the Okies could find a way to survive in a society that rejected them. Joe, in a burst of eloquence and passion, described a new society that would guarantee jobs, banish poverty, educate all, provide housing for everyone, and end discrimination against Negroes, Jews, Catholics, labor union members. He called his society *socialism*. He not only kept me awake: he woke me up.

In time I became a believer in socialism as a society that would benefit all the people. I came to believe that being a part of a movement, a vast brotherhood, to establish a just, humane and peace-loving society was to live a full and fruitful life.

6

DIXIE LOU

"**I** admire you," I said.

We were sprawled on the oriental rug in her living room, our backs to the ornately-carved antique couch. I caressed the silky wisps of hair on her arms.

She raised her head and shook it to get some of the mass of red hair out of her eyes.

"You would?" she asked.

I frowned. *You would?* I didn't understand. I say…I admire you. She says…you would? Makes no sense.

We were both twenty-two, seniors. I a journalism major, she majoring in drama and dance. I met her when I wrote publicity stories for the play in which she had a leading role.

The first time I saw her was in the university auditorium on a wintry afternoon. I wore a black woolen coat almost to my ankles. She stood center stage, ready to read from a script. Above me, on the back-lighted stage, her red hair glowing, she was a towering Venus.

"Who are you?" she asked. She tossed her hair back, leaned forward slightly. She wore a tight-fitting cashmere sweater, flared skirt and saddle shoes—the uniform of coeds of 1940.

My heart pounded. I felt my face smolder. My eyes weren't focusing. All I could see were rounded breasts under a pink sweater and long strands of glistening red hair.

I'm doing publicity for this play, I told her. She looked down at me with an interest I'd never before seen in the eyes of a woman.

"Good," she said. "I really want to see more of you."

I blushed again. An immense pleasure rolled through me. No woman had ever singled me out this way, this directly. I took my coat off and watched her. In a moment, she transformed herself into a troubled, anxious old woman. Moving stiffly, her body bent, her strained face shifting with each declamation like images on a motion picture screen. Her voice, strong and throaty, sounded authentically quavery to me; her cashmere sweater jiggled with each sweep of her arms.

I'd never encountered a woman like her. Sure, I'd had dates, blind and wide-eyed, in high school, and some at the university. But I'd been uncomfortable and artificial with them. Here was a woman who liked me, who made it known. I didn't have to prove myself.

She later told me about herself: her name was Dixie Lou; she was the adopted daughter of a politician, now chairman of the Ohio Public Works Commission. He'd lived in Columbus since his wife's death a few years back, and Dixie was being looked after by a housekeeper in the old family residence in Athens, a half-mile from campus. She didn't know who her parents were; she imagined, perhaps hoped, that her mother had been a student at Ohio State University in Columbus and her father a soldier on his way to war in France. She had memories of her adoptive mother, who died while she was in high school, but few words about her politician father, whom she saw only on his rare trips to Athens.

After rehearsals Dixie Lou and I walked home together. I couldn't afford to treat her to a milkshake at the Dairy Queen, the campus hangout. She was happy to stretch out on the rug with me in the living room of her home—a room of stately sideboards, ornate end tables and lace-curtained windows. We didn't sit on the red plush couch because Dixie said it was a family treasure that had to be preserved. (I sat on it once. The old springs almost punctured me.)

I opened up for the first time in my life. I talked about my feelings, my dreams, about my parents and how they didn't understand me, about my newfound radicalism. I felt listened to, believed in. I could even believe in myself as an articulate and mature man, not a boy.

With our backs propped against the couch, we wrapped our arms around each other and kissed, clutched, stroked, twisted, and rolled until we heard keys fumbling in the lock: It was the housekeeper returning with a load of groceries. We untangled quickly. I scrambled to pick up my books and at the door met Mrs. Barrow, the house-keeper—her mouth tight with disapproval.

"Thanks for studying with me," I said offhandedly to Dixie, hoping to divert the housekeeper's suspicions.

"I'd better go to my job now. I'll be late." I backed out the door.

AND SO IT WENT for many weeks. The kisses became longer and sweeter, the embraces closer and more feverish, the passion flowing like magnetic electrons from one to the other as we rolled on the rug—especially when Mrs. Barrow was out shopping. Other days we sat with a book between us and I held her arms and stroked, long and gently.

"You know the first day we met?" she asked. "You walked into the hall with that black coat of yours. You looked like some dark bird...an eagle swooping down...your black hair and black eyebrows coming out of the cloak. It was as if you were swooping down to snatch me up and carry me away." She shivered a little at the memory and leaned against me.

I sighed and continued to run my hands up and down her arms and to her shoulders. Dare I caress her breasts, that with each meeting seemed to swell before my eyes?

No. No, you don't. I remembered the words of advice by my mother (my mother, not my father!): "You don't take advantage of nice girls."

I continued to massage Dixie Lou's shoulders. How else do you respond to someone who says you're an eagle swooping down to snatch her away?

"I admire you," I muttered. I couldn't say, "I *love you.*" I didn't know what love was. In all my life no one had said to me, "I love you," and I'd never said "I love you" to anyone—mother, father, brothers, cousins. All I knew of love was the impersonal version in the movies.

Was this mad rushing of the blood love? Was the swelling penis love? Was this pulsing ache love? Was the straining, sweating, rising fever of the entire body love?

"I admire you," I mumbled.

And she replied, "You would?" her voice rising incredulously.

"You would what?" I finally asked.

"Marry me."

I stared at her thin, intense face, at her tongue nervously licking the corners of her lips, at the freckles at the end of her nose. My mind was cottony; there was a muffled pounding in the ears.

Marry? How did she get *marry* out of I admire you?

Say it slowly. With a Brooklyn accent. Growl it out between your teeth. Swallow the words: *I'dmirre you.*

The language of love.

"Sure," I said. "Why not?"

"Oh, Mel," she shrieked and hugged me fiercely, throwing me back to the rug, kissing my lips, my cheeks, my forehead. "Oh, Mel, I love you. I love you."

Overwhelmed, I whispered, "I love you, too, Dixie."

THERE. I SAID IT. It was sealed. *I love you.* First time I ever said it. Love writ large, writ forever. It had been pledged, vowed and branded onto my burning flesh.

We kissed again, tenderly, gently.

"Oh, Mel," she breathed in my ear, "Let's do it right away."

Let's do it now, I thought. I closed my legs tightly to keep the tumescence from showing.

"Let's go to Kentucky and find a Justice of the Peace."

"Kentucky? Why Kentucky? Why not here?"

"Cause Kentucky doesn't have a waiting period. And you don't need a test."

"How do you know all this stuff?"

"Oh, I talked to some girls who did it. You never know when you need this kind of information."

"How we going to get to Kentucky?"

"Well, we could take a bus…But that takes too long."

I stared at her, stretched beside me, chin propped in her hand, reeling out plans on the screen of her mind.

"Hey. I got it. Why don't you borrow Michael's car?"

"Michael Murphy's?"

"Yes."

"It's not his car. It belongs to his wife."

"Same thing."

I looked at her again. There was a certainty in her not to be denied.

Michael Murphy was the new general assignment reporter on *The Athens Messenger*. He and I and his wife, Eleanor, had become friends. We'd been to a few lectures, had a few beers together and swapped some stories. Hardly enough to ask them to trust you with their car. Yet, they *did* have a car.

"I'll ask them tomorrow."

"No. Right now."

It was late in the afternoon. She knew Michael finished his work at two on the paper.

"Okay. I'll walk over to his apartment."

"Good. I'll pack some things."

It was surprisingly easy. I asked to borrow the car for a couple of days. Why? they asked. Because Dixie Lou and I want to get married in Kentucky, I replied. Oh, yes, Eleanor sighed.

They were newly married themselves and full of romance. "Oh, how exciting," Eleanor said, glancing up at Michael, who gave me a questioning look: Do you know what you're doing? I ignored the look as he handed me the key.

"Fill it up with gas when you bring it back," he said curtly.

As I started the car, a two-door Ford sedan, his tone became an admonition. Gas costs money. Where do I get the money for gas? Or for a marriage license? And I wasn't going to drive the 120 miles to Kentucky and back in one night. Where do I get enough for a hotel room, a honeymoon suite? For breakfast, for dinner?

I mentioned these worries to Dixie when I drove back. "I've got to borrow some money somewhere."

"Oh, don't worry about it." She peered in the hallway mirror and swept a comb through her hair. "I've plenty of money."

"But I've got to leave a note for Mrs. Barrow," she said, her brow furrowing. "What do I say?" She dabbed a lipstick at the bow in her lips. "I can't say I've gone to Kentucky to elope. She'll have a fit. And she'll call Daddy." She licked a fingertip and ran it over an eyebrow, staring at herself intently.

"I know. I'll tell her I'm staying over at Betty Jane's for the week-end." A smile of satisfaction came to her lips as she licked her finger again and rubbed the other eyebrow.

I DROVE UP MOUND STREET to the top of the hill and the small house where I lived with three other students. "I've got to get into my suit. I can't get married in these clothes." She waited in the car.

"What in the hell are you doing?" asked Bloomy as I heaped clothes into a small suitcase. Bloomy was Leonard Blumen, with whom I'd roomed for three years; we were buddies and helpmates.

"I'm getting married," I mumbled, stuffing a pair of socks and toothbrush into the case. "I borrowed Michael's car and we're going to Kentucky right now."

"*Married? Kentucky?*" His dark eyes seemed to be popping through his tortoise-shell glasses, making him look more a scholar than he was. He sat in a chair, watching me pack. "Who to?"

"Dixie Lou Williams."

"Dixie Lou," he sputtered. "Dixie Lou, the whore of Athens! Are you crazy? What in hell is the matter with you?"

"Whore? What are you talking about? Where did you get that shit? Whore! She's no whore."

"Boy, you don't know much, do you?"

"I know she's a helluva nice girl. And I love her." I pounded the suitcase shut.

"Nice," Bloomy roared back. "Nice. Nice enough to fuck the whole basketball team."

"That's a lie. A goddamned lie. I've been with her every day for weeks. Nobody's been fucking her. Not even me."

"That's how much you know. Everybody in town knows that you can knock on her window, climb into her room and screw the hell out of her. Everybody knows it. Except you."

"What a goddamned lie. Bloomy, why are you doing this to me? Why are you spreading this malicious gossip? Have you ever fucked her?"

"No."

"Then you're just a goddamn lying gossip. You can go fuck *yourself*. I hope I never see you again."

I stumbled to the car and threw the suitcase in the back seat, my hands trembling as I gripped the steering wheel.

"What's the matter, Mel? What happened?" she asked.

"Nothing. Bloomy got me mad."

"Don't stay mad." She edged across the seat and leaned her head against my shoulder. "This is a happy time. Time of our life."

I turned the key. The motor shook for a moment, coughed to a start and chugged and throbbed: *Lie...Lie...Lie...*

WE HEADED WEST on U.S. 50 to Chillicothe, through hilly countryside, green and lush in the late springtime, and through villages and towns brushed rose and purple by the sun's setting rays. My anger drifted away as the car hummed along on the smooth two-lane highway. We climbed Rattlesnake Knob and rolled downhill to Chillicothe in the dusk, then turned south to Portsmouth, another fifty or so miles.

In the dark, Dixie began singing and humming softly, leaning beside me. Her sweet voice and the rhythm of the rolling tires and whistling wind and the drone of the motor set my mind free. I held the wheel and steered the car automatically.

Marriage. You get a job. The wife stays home, cleans house, washes your clothes. Has a baby. Takes care of the baby and you. Is that it? What do I really know about marriage? Nothing. Except the one I came out of.

I shuddered.

The fights. Yelling and screaming and crying and wailing. Head covered with stifling pillows to escape what you can't escape: the heavy voice of my father, quavering angrily; my mother's imploring sobs; the sudden banging of the door and then the silence, the oppressive silence.

I looked down at Dixie, now dozing on her back with her head on my thigh, her legs braced against the car door.

All marriages couldn't be like that. Marriages couldn't last. No one would get married. But they do. Why? Not just to propagate. Not just for sex.

Dixie moved her head, turning her body on the seat, curling her knees up and shifting her hand to my thigh. I could feel a swelling, and my pants suddenly became tight.

Well, it could be. That would be nice. Getting it…anytime. Oh, God. Anytime you wanted it. No more blue balls. Come home to a sweet-smelling body. Oh, my God. To be next to her…naked…feeling her breasts…

I shivered. The car swerved as my hands shook. I glanced down at Dixie, who stirred in her sleep.

But what if it didn't go in? What if I didn't know how? I've never done it before. Maybe there's a special way. And I don't know that special way. Goddamn, What am I going to do?

A cold chill swept through me. I found myself needing air, lots of air, and I rolled the window down to gulp at the rush. Dixie raised her head, groped her way up to a seated position and rubbed her eyes.

"We almost there?" she asked with a yawn.

I swallowed hard a few times. "Couple of miles more to the bridge. But I don't know where we go once we cross the river."

"I do. Go to this little town called Firebrick. It's not far."

"What's at Firebrick?"

"A Justice of the Peace, silly."

"It's pretty late. How do you know he'll be open?"

"He's always open."

"How do you know?"

"I know. One of my girlfriends told me."

I shook my head in disbelief and eased my foot on the accelerator as we bumped over the wood and steel trestle that crossed the Ohio River.

THE CAR'S HEADLIGHTS flickered over the road sign announcing Firebrick, and a moment later over another sign swinging from a post beside a gate in a white picket fence. "W.R. Plant. Justice of the Peace." Cicadas screeched and frogs grumbled in chorus, the only sounds in the town.

We stood in the dark and stared at the grey house set back from the fence.

"There's nobody home. Or they're all asleep," I said. "Let's come back in the morning."

"Wait. I see someone at the window."

She went up the walk. I followed as she climbed three steps to the porch and knocked softly on the door. A light went on and the door opened tentatively.

A tall man, hurriedly stuffing a white shirt into his pants and adjusting his suspenders, peered through the half-open door. "You need help?" he asked in a strained voice.

"We'd like to get married," Dixie said. "Tonight."

"Wa'll it's kinda late. But let me see if we can accommodate you." He turned from the door and shuffled away. His slippers, tapping on the hard floor, sounded like cicadas.

He returned in a few moments to open the door wide. "Come in. Come in." He turned on a light, a bare bulb dangling from an electric cord, in the hall. "Wait in here." He pointed to the living room and switched on a lamp in the corner. "My wife and daughter will be down in a few minutes. You need witnesses, you know."

Gaunt and hollow-cheeked, hair disheveled and eyes deep-set and dark, W. R. Plant had the look of a fiery preacher. He nodded toward a couch in front of a bay window. "You can sit down."

The cracked-leather couch was dwarfed by a large battered desk from which W.R. Plant conducted his business. On the wall behind the desk were dozens of framed photographs, diplomas and citations, and a clothes rack on which hung a black alpaca coat, its sleeves dangling stiffly, as if arms remained in them.

Still in his slippers, W.R. Plant shuffled around the desk, arranging paper in orderly rows and lifting a large Bible from a drawer. He buttoned his shirt, slipped his coat on, sat down, pulled a folder from another drawer, plucked out a sheet of paper, and picked up a pen.

"I need some information," he began. "First, your name and age." He turned to Dixie.

"Mary Jane McConahay," she said, her face flushing. She glanced at me. "I'm twenty-two."

What's going on here, I wondered. I squirmed on the couch and turned to face Dixie Lou.

"Address?"

"72 State Street, Chillicothe, Ohio."

Why's she lying? I asked myself. What's she doing?

I stood up abruptly. "I'm going outside for a minute. I need a smoke."

W.R. Plant looked up at me. "Nervous, huh? That's understandable."

On the porch I leaned against a pillar and listened to the cicadas. I took some deep breaths to smother the pounding in my head. I didn't smoke, but I wished I had a cigarette or a drink. *What in hell is she doing? Why?*

Dixie came through the door. "He's ready for you now," she said.

"Why'd you give him another name?" I hissed. "Why'd you give him a false address?"

"I don't want Daddy to find out," she whispered. "The papers report all marriage licenses. His friends in Portsmouth would tell him if they saw that Dixie Lou Williams of Athens got a license."

"Should I do it too?"

"Maybe you should. Someone in Athens might get suspicious."

"What name should I use?"

She shrugged. "Come on."

We returned to the room, where a heavy-set woman in a flowered print cotton dress now stood stiffly beside a big-bosomed younger woman in a white blouse and flared skirt. Mother and daughter. Both wore scarves over hair bound in pin-curlers. The daughter yawned, covering her mouth with a thick hand.

W. R. Plant introduced them and picked up his pen. "Name and age?" "Paul Faris. Twenty-two," I replied. Paul, the name of my good friend from high school days, and Faris, my mother's maiden name.

"Address?"

"33 Mound Street, Nelsonville, Ohio."

There. The lying was complete. We were united in lies. Next, marriage.

W.R. Plant stood behind the desk, Mary Jane and Paul before him, mother and daughter to the left, nearest the door leading to the hall and the stairs going up to their bedrooms.

"Do you, Mary Jane, take this man, Paul, to be your lawfully wedded husband...." he droned, his head bent to read from the Bible before him on the desk.

"I do."

"Do you, Paul, take this woman, Mary Jane..."

"I do."

"I hereby declare you man and wife." He lifted his head, his lips stretched in a smile revealing yellowed teeth. "Good luck to you both. May you live happily ever after."

His wife and daughter murmured congratulations, excused themselves and fled upstairs.

W. R. Plant looked at us expectantly. "That'll be fifteen dollars," he said. He pulled his rickety swivel chair to the desk, sat down and began filling in the blanks of an official-looking marriage certificate.

Dixie turned away, dug into her purse, and thrust the bills into my hands. I stepped around her and left the money on the desk.

"Thanks," W.R. Plant mumbled. He stood, handed me the certificate and escorted us to the door.

The cicadas and bullfrogs greeted us with their version of "The Wedding March."

I SIGNED THE PORTSMOUTH HOTEL REGISTER with a flourish: "Mr. and Mrs. Paul Faris." If they doubted it, I could pull out the marriage certificate and show them. But the desk clerk turned the book toward him, and, with pen poised over the Paid column, said: "That'll be ten dollars, please."

A young bellboy carried our bags up three flights and opened the door to a high-ceilinged room with a large double bed. He ran a practiced eye over Dixie Lou as he placed our suitcases beside a dresser. She sat on the bed, testing it with slight jumps. Her hair flew around her shoulders and her white shirtwaist blouse billowed. The bellboy stood at the door, staring fixedly at her, his mouth open. I did too, until I realized he was waiting for a tip. I gave him a quarter and eased him through the door.

I turned to Dixie. My head burned. My body was on fire. I shook with anticipation, with joy and delight, with fear. My throat was dry. I couldn't talk.

I crossed the room, took her hand, pulled her to her feet and embraced her, running my hands over her back, feeling her shiver, feeling her press insistently against me with her hips, tasting her tongued kisses.

She reached up and undid my jacket and helped me pull the coat from my shoulders and arms. I pushed her hands away, clumsily unbuttoned my shirt, pulled off my pants and stood trembling before her in my underwear.

She slowly unbuttoned her blouse, peeling it off even more slowly, revealing a thin net brassiere that barely enclosed her breasts.

I stood transfixed.

She undid her skirt, stooping down to step out of it. Her breasts dangled before my eyes. She drew her underpants slowly down her thighs and her legs. A mound of golden red emerged and she stood before me in all her glory.

Boiling point!

I tore my underwear off, my penis rigid and quivering between us.

I eased her back to the bed and with fevered haste leaned over her, holding my penis in my hand, trying to find the secret place with its cover of golden down.

I burst out of my skin and gushed in a huge spurt over her.

"Oh, Mel," she cried despairingly. "Couldn't you wait?"

I shook my head and lowered myself to the bed beside her. "I couldn't help it," I whispered. "I don't know what happened. I just couldn't help it. I've never done it before."

"Oh, my God," she said, her eyes widening. "You're a virgin."

She laughed raucously, derisively. "Oh, my God. I got a virgin." She laughed again, short, spasmodic gasps, covering her mouth with the back of her hand, then turning and burying her head in a pillow.

7

ON THE ROAD

I hitchhiked down the Ohio Valley and across southern West Virginia in the summer of 1940, approaching editors in newspaper city rooms, sometimes standing in long lines to fill out applications in factories and mills, looking for work—any work. Times were tough, I was constantly reminded, and I kept getting turned down. Twenty million other people and me.

I didn't try to find a job in a filling station, because I wanted to put my journalism training to use. Besides, a newspaper job paid better than pumping gas at twenty-five cents an hour, the minimum wage then.

With a canvas suitcase in one hand and an out-thrust thumb on the other, I found rides to factory towns along the Ohio River. Usually, I was let off near the center of town. In grubby gas station toilets I stripped off my road clothes, washed up, and put on my wrinkled blue serge suit to appear presentable when I accosted an editor.

As the editor looked up from his desk, I'd tell him I'd studied journalism at Ohio University and had worked on *The Athens Messenger* for a couple of years. I'd ask hastily if he had a reporter's job open. Some responded brusquely, some kindly. Some were solicitous, some helpful. But they all said no.

Disappointed, I'd leave the newspaper and hunt out a restaurant. From a small change purse, I'd extract five cents for a cup of coffee. As unobtrusively as possible, I spooned sugar into the coffee until it was saturated. The warm, liquid sugar was my meal for the afternoon, and often for the evening.

If it was late, I'd call it a day, head to another gas station to change my clothes, fold my suit into the canvas case, then walk to a residential street off the main highway until I found a parked car and sat near it, waiting for nightfall. When all was quiet on the street and lights flickered out in the houses, I'd open the car door and crawl into the back, stretching out on the seat, the plush roof sloping over me protectively, like a small tent. I curled up on the seat, my suitcase a pillow, counting on daylight to awaken me before the owner returned. I was stealing sleep; it beat sleeping in cold, wet fields.

My days started early, when dawn came through the car windows. Stiff, groggy, I'd walk to a cafe, wash up, order coffee and, if there was any extra change in the purse, a doughnut. Then the road.

Morning rides seldom took me far. Men going to work carried me short distances. One morning, though, south of Huntington, I caught a ride with a hardware salesman on his way to Williamson, sixty miles over mountain roads. He drove a two-door Ford, its back seat crammed with shovels, axes, rakes and other tools.

Dressed in a rumpled black suit, he was gaunt, his neck taut and stringy, his Adams apple protruding like a beak. His eyes left the road for a second as he peered sideways at me. He asked where I was headed.

I told him I was trying to find a job on a newspaper, explaining that I'd been studying journalism in college.

He grunted. He told me in a nasal twang that there were sparse pickings down the road. He ticked off Williamson, Welch, Bluefield, maybe Princeton, adding that he knew those towns well. His customers included two or three stores in each city as well as company stores "in the hollers."

Holler? Did I dare show my ignorance and ask? I did.

He squinted at me. "Holler? Why that's a place—a bunch of houses. With a store. Near a mine. 'Tween a couple of mountains."

I nodded, as if I understood.

Suddenly, in a voice cracked with dryness, he blurted angry words about company stores and the coal companies that owned them. He sputtered on about how miners in those towns were forced to pay high prices for his hardware and other goods in those stores. Then, just as suddenly, he stopped. He asked himself what he was griping about. "I've got a job. Helluva a lot better than most people, ain't it?"

I nodded and squirmed to control the rumblings in my stomach. I was afraid they were loud enough to be heard by the salesman. I coughed and cleared my throat to hide each rumble.

The tires made sucking noises on the hot tar of the road. The tools in the back clanked and rattled as the car bounced over ruts and potholes. The salesman began braking as he rounded a curve and saw a rough cabin beside the road. A crudely-lettered sign announced "EATS" from the eaves.

Twisting his mouth in a wry grin, he told me he was hungry, that I was hungry, and that we should get "some eats."

I can still taste that feast: half a chicken, steak-fried, mashed potatoes drowned in gravy, fried tomatoes, biscuits with jam, endless coffee without sugar. I sat on a stool next to the salesman and ate deliberately, relishing the good taste, the smell, the abundance.

He watched me unhurriedly. He shook his head as I cleaned the plate with bits of biscuit. While I tipped my coffee cup back to get the last drop, he pulled a dollar bill from a small roll in his pocket and paid for his meal and mine. Eighty-five cents.

I thanked him as we settled back in the car. Twenty miles to Williamson, he announced.

Sooty red-brick buildings lined the dusty main street when we got there. The salesman parked in front of a hardware store and stepped out of the car. He reached into his pocket.

Thrusting two quarters into my hand, he told me that he knew what it was like to be hungry. He'd been there, too. He told me to get something to eat later and turned away.

I thanked him and watched him carry a battered briefcase and a box into the store. "Good luck," he called back.

I followed my routine of changing into a suit to hear another editor say no. After I switched to my traveling clothes, I hurried to the city's outskirts and stood beside a U.S. Route 52 sign. It was mid-afternoon. I could get in a few more miles before dark.

THE CAR THAT STOPPED NEXT was a brand-new Hudson sedan. The driver, his weather-beaten face peppered with specks and pock-marks, announced he was going as far as Welch.

White paper was spread on the car seat. I slid in beside the driver, who quickly told me the Hudson wasn't his—that he was delivering it to a dealer in Welch. I sat back, luxuriating in the comfort and enjoy-ing the new car aroma, just as fine then as it is today.

He said he wanted to get to Welch in time to catch the last bus back to Williamson; he drove fast, skidding around curves, and jamming down the accelerator on straight-aways. He slowed only through the grimy, meager coal towns. Company stores, which also housed the coal company offices, the police force, post office and the company doctor's clinic, dominated the main streets of these coal-blackened towns. Every ten miles or so another town bulged in the road.

The driver kept up a commentary. "This here's Pie," he reported as we came to bleak clapboarded buildings facing the road and two rows of railroad tracks. He didn't know how it got that name. "It ain't pie in the sky," he chuckled. "That's for sure."

Justice was a town in a narrow valley severed by a deeply-rutted dirt road. Rickety houses, some on gangling stilts, clung to the steep hill-sides. Behind the shacks were narrow outhouses. No justice there, my driver opined.

When we came to a town called Iaeger he slowed the car to a crawl. He was raised here "in Yayger," he said, and got his first job in the mines when he was fifteen. Now I knew what the specks on his face were—coal dust embedded in his skin.

He explained that the coal seams hereabouts were sometimes three feet thick. You had to crawl in to get it and "crawl around like a snake to shovel it out," he said. His shoulders twitched, as if shuddering over a buried fear. He confessed that work in the mines "got to me." He couldn't crawl into any more holes, he said. "I needed space."

He slapped the steering wheel. "I got lucky," he laughed. "Got me this garage job in Williamson." He jammed his foot down on the accelerator. The car lurched past the Iaeger company store. He told me, with a shake of his head, that he probably would still be working in the mines if the seams had been thicker, as they were in Welch.

He drove deftly around hairpin turns as the road curved between steep mountain slopes. Abruptly, the road dropped into Welch, a city in a bowl of mountains.

Wyoming Street, narrow and paved with cracked red brick, went past the county courthouse, a four-story granite building on top of a hill. Blocks of granite steps led up to the courthouse entrance where two torch-like lights punctured the dusk. I shivered a little in the sudden cold as I got out of the car and thanked my driver.

Too late to visit the Welch *Daily News* across from the courthouse, I wandered along dingy Main Street, past a department store called Robinson's, past a marble-fronted jewelry shop, a narrow telephone company building, two banks on opposite sides of the street, and around the corner to a restaurant I remember as the Acropolis. Its lights were a beacon.

THE SIGN IN THE WINDOW attracted me: "All you can eat—50 cents." I *had* 50 cents. And I was hungry again. I opened the fly-specked screen door. A short, dark-haired man in a white apron stood behind a linoleum-covered counter, wiping it down.

He watched me as I sat at a counter stool. "Coffee?" he asked, reaching for a cup and saucer. I nodded. He went to a stove against the back wall near the end of the counter and filled the cup from a battered coffee pot.

I asked him if I could get steak and potatoes for fifty cents.

"All you can eat," he replied. "Like the sign says."

While he went to the stove to fill my order, I looked around. A few tables along a wall faced the counter and its line of stools. On the wall was an idealized representation of the real Acropolis, surrounded by swirling clouds, on a denuded Athenian hill. Most of the painting was clouds.

I soon found out that his name was Gus. He told me about himself as he bustled around his pots and pans. He was, of course, from Greece, and had come to Welch because a cousin of his, a miner, had paid his way. After working for years in restaurants, he opened his own, becoming independent and proud in America.

He brought the browned steak, flanked by mashed potatoes and bedraggled green beans and set it before me with a flourish. He stepped back and folded his arms across his chest, observing me like an anxious mother.

I'd told him I was going to apply for a job on the *Daily News* the next morning, and he said that I might get a job because things were picking up. He began wiping the counter compulsively. "This is the Billion-Dollar Coalfield," he informed me, his voice rising excitedly. "McDowell County *is* the Billion-Dollar Coalfield," he repeated, as if considering himself a part owner, savoring his share of the billion.

I nodded and chewed in agreement.

Gus chattered on, his dialect part Greek, part mountaineer. He suggested I try the mines if the job at the *News* didn't come through. The mines were hiring, he said.

I cut the juicy steak, stirred it around in the gravy and shoveled it into my mouth. That was the only shoveling I wanted to do, but I didn't tell him that.

I cleaned my plate and pushed it toward Gus. He went back to the big stove, returning with another steak, more potatoes and beans. Leaning up against the counter, he stood watch.

Slowly I chewed on the meat and nibbled on the beans. Suddenly I felt something erupting within me.

"Where's the toilet, Gus?" I muttered. He pointed. I stumbled to the door, opened it and plunged my head toward the bowl. I heaved. I retched up steak, potatoes, beans, chicken, biscuits and doughnuts, back to the beginning of time.

Finally, I washed my face with cold water, cleaned the bowl and staggered to my seat at the counter. Gus sympathetically handed me a cup of tea. It warmed the hole in my stomach. I stopped shaking.

I slapped my two quarters on the counter as I thanked Gus and apologized for the mess I made. I picked up my suitcase, headed to the door and asked where the bus station was.

He came to the door, grabbed my arm and put the two quarters in my hand. He held my shirt sleeve, warning me that the police wouldn't let me sleep in the bus station.

He stepped aside to let a couple through the door to the restaurant. "Come back later," he said. "Sleep in my place." He turned to his customers.

I looked at Gus as he stood behind his counter. Three large bulbs overhead lit the restaurant as if it were a stage set. Gus was center front, his broad face and crinky hair spotlighted. What made a man like him so generous? Was it sentiment for strangers such as he, in a strange land? Was it a need to be accepted in this alien place? I wondered about Gus and all the good, helpful people I'd met on the road.

I dozed fitfully on the cold courthouse steps until dark and then returned to the Acropolis. Gus offered me some food. I refused, but drank tea while he stacked chairs on tabletops and swept up. Tucking a small cash box under his arm, he led me past the courthouse, up a small hill and down a driveway to a house terraced into the side of another hill. Ducking between wooden posts that held up the back of the house, Gus opened a door into a basement apartment. The sitting room into which we walked held two overstuffed chairs and a dark green velour couch. The place was neat and warm.

Gus pointed to a doorway, grinned and said, "Bathroom." He waved me to his couch and went to a closet-like kitchen to boil water for more tea, which we savored as he talked about his life. I sat back on the couch, listening, but the warmth of the apartment and events of the day and weeks caught up with me. I fell asleep sitting upright.

Gus woke me while it was still dark. He had to be in his restaurant at five. I washed up quickly, put on my good suit, and followed him through the murky dawn. At the counter I ate a stack of pancakes and watched Gus feed a steady stream of customers as they shuffled in. When I saw black-rimmed eyes I knew they were coal miners.

PROMPTLY AT EIGHT, I was in the Welch *Daily News* building, reading yesterday's paper, waiting for the editor. He led me upstairs to his small office, lifted newspapers and books from a chair and invited me to sit. "I'm Will Keyser," he said, extending a bony hand. Greying hair, cut short, framed a high forehead. He examined me through rimless glasses.

I explained how I happened to be in Welch, told him of my background, and showed him my book of clippings. He looked through the book carefully, reading all my stories.

Leaning back in his chair, he told me that a job was opening up in a week. "Our courthouse reporter is leaving to go back to school," he said. He handed back my book of clips. "You write clearly and simply," he said. "That's what we want."

Then he offered me the job. I think my heart stopped.

"The pay is $18 a week," he added. "And anytime you write over 200 inches in a week, I'll pay you a nickel an inch."

I did a quick calculation. If I worked 40 hours, that meant I made 45 cents an hour. A small fortune. And the extra five cents an inch. A bonanza.

I wanted to jump onto Will Keyser's cluttered desk and do a jig. But I stood up, leaned over, took his hand and solemnly promised to do a good job. He suggested we meet the city editor, Kid Hardison, and the rest of his staff. I nodded, somewhat dazed, followed him out of the office, and stopped him in the hallway.

I told him, apologetically, that I didn't know how I could stay there for a week; I didn't have any money. "No," I added, "I've got 60 cents."

He looked at me, shrugged, and said he'd give me another job for the week. He turned to a door in the hallway and pulled it open. A rank, musty smell overwhelmed us as two large cartons crammed with clippings, mats and photographs tumbled out. Other boxes were piled from floor to ceiling beside overflowing file cabinets. A colossal mess.

He explained that this was the "morgue," newspaper talk for the *Daily News* reference and photograph files. He told me to spend the week organizing it, to do the best I could.

He reached for his wallet and pulled out a ten-dollar bill.

"Here's your pay in advance," he said.

Two weeks later, after getting my first pay envelope, I sent bus fare to Dixie Lou, who was waiting for me at a cousin's near Huntington. She found a tiny apartment, with kitchen, for eight dollars a week, and we somehow managed to feed ourselves on the remaining ten.

For the next fifteen months I covered the courthouse, state and city police, the draft board, City Hall, hospitals and mortuaries in Welch and nearby communities. I wrote about mine accidents—three of them major catastrophes—murders and murder trials, and the first contingent of World War II draftees, working with another reporter on local elections. Every day was exciting.

Once I learned my beat and was accepted by my sources, I churned out the stories, exceeding the 200-inch minimum many times. My pay envelopes often were $25 or more. One week, an election week, my pay was $38. Will Keyser called me in, told me I was doing very well and gave me a $2 raise, to $20 a week. But, he paused—a long pause—and said he'd have to cut out the five cents an inch.

A month or so later, I left to take a job as editor of the *Voice of Labor* in Cumberland, Maryland at $40 a week.

THE *VOICE OF LABOR* covered the activities of textile workers in the giant Celanese plant, rubber workers in the Kelly-Springfield Tire Co. factory, coal miners, and laundry and railroad workers in the hills of Western Maryland.

Ten thousand copies circulated weekly. I wrote and edited all the local stories, recruited the bartender in the saloon on the first floor of the labor hall building to write a sports column, rode the paper through the print shop, then distributed copies at the plant gates. A merry-go-round.

An old tennis pro was advertising manager, and Dixie Lou read proof sometimes—my only helpers.

I had a draft deferment because of my marriage to Dixie Lou, but after eighteen months of day-and-night rides on that carousel, I quit the paper and enlisted in the Marines in early 1943.

I was twenty-five: the oldest man in our platoon in boot camp. I weighed 134 pounds. At six feet three inches, I looked like a walking stick. Three months later, after huge infusions of meat and potatoes, I weighed 170, some of it muscle.

8

WARS

My younger brother mailed me a recent clipping from a Florida newspaper. The headline reads: AMERICANS PAY DEARLY FOR TINY CORAL ISLAND.

The story commemorates the fiftieth anniversary of the First Marine Division's landing on Peleliu.

Mort saw his three brothers go to war. He read and reread the letters we sent from the Marines, the Air Force and Navy. But when we came home, we didn't talk about the war—to him, to each other.

Is the story he sends a gentle reminder that it's all right to tell him how it was—to end the silence?

I hope so, Mort. That day, September 15, 1944, comes back to me in waves of fear and sorrow, much more than I want to remember....

It's as the newspaper story says: *Ten thousand Japanese soldiers and sailors greet them with a rain of gunfire. It's a bad beginning that will only get worse.*

I'm on the troop transport *S.S. Sea Runner* with five hundred Marines. We watch black smoke and debris shoot up from the shores. Most of us look anxiously at this onshore movie. Some clean rifles, sharpen bayonets and jungle knives. Some check packs and gear. Some just stare. But all are waiting for the call: to go down the nets into open boats to the beaches.

A tiny piece of coral sticking out of the Pacific Ocean in the Palau Islands, Peleliu is six miles long and two miles wide. Discovered by the Spanish explorer Villalobos in 1543, the island is claimed by Spain, but never was developed. The Japanese, awarded the Palaus from Germany after World War I, turn Peleliu into a forward military base. Admiral Chester Nimitz, commander of all Navy forces in the Pacific, covets Peleliu's airfield.

Gripping the rail of the *Sea Runner*, my buddy Mickey and I watch Navy torpedo bombers take off sluggishly from nearby aircraft carriers, skipping their bombs on the island as if they were flat stones on a lake. Four days and nights of bombing pockmark and crater the hills, stripping the tops from coconut palms and shredding the green jungle vines. These hills loom now, bare and white in the blazing sun.

The diving, screeching planes, the swishing salvos of rockets blasting out of gunships, and the pounding of sixteen-inch guns from the battleships lined up close by make me shudder, make my head ache.

My stomach knots in fear as I watch Japanese shells, fired from guns in the hills, blow up small boats, the huge plumes of white water mixed with dark specks of bodies and boat fragments. My fate, too?

One burly Marine in my platoon, Ted, a deputy sheriff from Kansas, breaks away from the rail. "I'm not going," his voice a screech. "I'm not going. Get me outta here." He drops to the iron deck, shaking and sobbing, scratching for a hand-hold that will keep him on the ship. He flails while the gunnery sergeant and lieutenant jump on him and wrestle him off the deck. He screams and curses as they drag him to the ship's brig.

I watch this struggle in silence, recognizing how close I am, how close we all are, to cracking under such panic and fright. Here I am, I remember thinking, watching black smoke rising from the island, white geysers shooting up from the roiling ocean, the buzz of gnat-like bombers, the ear-shattering blasts of naval guns—and we're about to go over the side of this ship into that bloody inferno. Ted didn't go mad; *we're* mad.

We're trained to be mad, to turn off our feelings, to follow orders and think of nothing but duty, patriotism and *Semper Fi,* the Marine slogan translated in boot camp as "I got mine; fuck you, Buddy." From the moment you step off the train at Parris Island, South Carolina you obey orders. Drill instructors bark commands that often make no sense: get down on hands and knees and clean the barracks floor with a toothbrush, even if it takes all night. It's called *instilling discipline.* Actually it's intimidation, and that's its purpose: Follow orders. Don't question. Do it. Shut up. Do it because the sergeant, the lieutenant, the captain, the colonel, the general, the admiral order you to.

I ENLISTED IN THE MARINE Corps for three reasons. I'd been "promised" an assignment as combat correspondent by a general to whom I'd written. After I completed boot camp, he replied, he would arrange my transfer to that special unit of newspapermen he commanded. Second, ever since my days in high school, as Hitler bullied his way to power and Jew-hating spread in Germany and America, I'd been taunted and told "Jews can't fight." I joined to dispel that belief. Third, I wanted to help defeat German and Japanese fascism and help democracy flower in the world.

It was in boot camp that I learned I would have to fight the Jew-haters in the Marine Corps first. I was one of three Jewish men in the platoon. One day, after the platoon was ordered to stand at attention for more than an hour for some infraction of discipline, I heard an Italian kid from Brooklyn say, "It's those Jews. They always fuck things up for us." While the rest of the platoon sat nodding in agreement on their bunks I grabbed the kid around the waist, pinning his arms. I pushed my face into his. "You're one guy who should know better," I hissed. "That's what the Nazis say." I squeezed the breath out of him and pushed him against the bunk. He shook his head. "Sorry," he said. "I didn't mean it." That evening almost every member of the platoon came to me and apologized for the kid's outburst. I'd won a little battle.

After four months of rigorous training, including weeks on the firing range, I learned about *Semper Fidelis* first hand. The general refused my request for a transfer to his unit. Maybe he'd gotten word from the FBI that I was a radical because of my background as editor of the Western Maryland *Voice of Labor*.

Though on the rifle range I had the worst score of anyone in our boot platoon, I was declared a rifleman and assigned to a company of replacements headed for Guadalcanal. Four hundred of us boarded a new LST (Landing Ship, Tank) in New Orleans, headed south into the Caribbean and through the Panama Canal to the Pacific. After sixty days we dropped anchor at Bora Bora, near Tahiti, where we took on fresh water. Six days later we were dumped in Pago Pago, the deepwater port in American Samoa. The voyage had been an idyllic time, as I came to see later.

Except for its swarms of mosquitoes and the hard work we did loading and unloading ammunition from ship to ship, Samoa also was idyllic. My platoon became an anti-aircraft battery in a native village near a beach on the eastern end of the island. We'd been sidetracked to Samoa because our replacement company was needed neither in Guadalcanal nor in Tarawa, where a bloody battle had been raging as the LST zig-zagged its way across the Pacific.

I lived with five other men in a grass hut, a *fale*, near a long scope used to track planes. Surrounding our little group of huts were the larger native *fales*. A high and open community building made of columns of palm trunks and thatched with shafts of palm leaves commanded the compound.

Though we lived with the Samoans as guests in their village, we rarely were invited to their feasts, dances, celebrations or church services. We observed their life as if we were passersby looking through a window. Except for the village elders, who worked a deal with the lieutenant for a supply of beer, the Samoans ignored us.

I watched Samoan men spear fish on the reef and thought I'd like to try it until I discovered that these were the same fish circling around under our one-hole latrine at the end of a boardwalk on the reef.

Other planned southwest Pacific invasions are scrubbed when American military leaders move up the amphibious assault on Leyte Island in the Philippines from Dec. 20 to Oct. 20. But Nimitz, advised to by-pass Peleliu, rejects the advice, and Peleliu is invaded as scheduled.

Off Peleliu, that night of September 15, as I grip the deck rail and watch tank guns flash on the beaches, tracers skitter in the air, and flares illuminate the end of the island near the airfield where the battle rages, I realize that the Marines on the *Sea Runner* are not going over the side. I say to Mickey, "We're not going to hit the beach at night." He nods. "Yeah," he says. "Saved by the bell."

I sit down, my back to the bulkhead, and look up at the stars, more stars than I've ever seen before, filling the sky with hard, brilliant light, and know I'll see another day. Maybe other days, because there are signs that we may not even go over the side tomorrow.

How can we tell? The night before you hit the beach, the Marines always furnish a good meal, like that last meal for the condemned prisoner on death row. The last supper is steak, fries, ice cream and cake—all you can eat. Such a meal isn't dished out tonight—just ordinary chow, something with beans.

I fall asleep on the deck, pillowing my head on my knapsack, my shoes tucked into my helmet, my rifle beside me. On deck, I can breathe; below, in troop quarters, Marines are packed in tiers of five—thirty-five or forty to a compartment. It smells like the monkey cages in a zoo. There's no air—just smoke, fart stench and sweat. If your bunk is the lowest one, next to the floor, you smell feet; if the highest, near the pipes, you're stifled in the rising cigarette smoke. But no matter where you bunk, you're surrounded by moans and groans, anguished cries, muttering, grinding teeth, coughing fits and constant snoring.

Maj. Gen. William Rupertus, First Marine Division Commander, rashly predicts that the Peleliu operation will be 'a quickie. Rough but fast.' The overconfident Rupertus tells war correspondents that the island will be secured 'in two days, three at the most.' He is wrong by more than two months.

I feel the ship move during the night. Almost silently, its anchor is lifted and it pulls away from the line of attack transports, battleships, carriers, destroyers and supply ships along the east side of the island. I sit near the bulkhead and watch Peleliu become a shadow under the glittering sky as the *Sea Runner* slowly makes its way north.

I wake Mickey stretched out beside me. "Why are we pulling away from the line?" I ask him. He shakes his head groggily and turns away. I look up at the stars for a while and drift off to sleep. I awake at dawn, when the ship's engines stop, to find we're anchored in a large bay sprinkled with small, rocky, vine-covered islands. A tongue of land, curving around a thin beach, stretches up into hills crowded with coconut palms and jungle vines. In the morning light, the islands glint as if their green foliage had just been applied by the brush of a master artist.

Word spreads quickly that we're close to a Japanese-held island called Babelthuap (pronounced *Babel-thwop*), some thirty miles north of Peleliu. We're a headquarters company, the Third Island Command, scheduled to go in September 18, D-3, three days after the initial landing, when Rupertus said the battle would be over. A higher-ranking general, recognizing Rupertus' prediction as wishful, calls in additional reserves.

Two companies leave the *Sea Runner* on LCVP's and amphibious tractors that crawl over the reefs. Our company stays aboard. I sun myself on the fantail or play high stakes chess with Mickey, to whom I already owe $16,000. From time to time I glance up from the board to relish the serenity of the vibrant little islands in the bay, all the while hearing the whine of planes and the thudding of guns and shells in the distance.

Rupertus will attack with three Marine regiments. He is offered a fourth, but turns it down, saying it isn't needed. Eight days into the fighting, a regiment of the Army's 81st Infantry "Wildcat" Division is rushed into battle.

At the end of two weeks, (D-16) I owe Mickey close to $20,000. "I'm going to open the fanciest whorehouse in Philly with the money," he says. "I'll let you in free." While my chess game hasn't improved, my tan has. To exist in the equatorial heat, I'm out on deck dressed in cut-down shorts from dawn to dusk, and go below deck only to eat in the mess hall or shave and shower in the head with its back-to-back rows of open toilets. The head is also the place to go if you can't sleep and want to read at three o'clock in the morning; its lights are on all the time.

I'm not the only one who can't sleep below. Many other Marines spread their blankets inside trucks parked on the deck. I've found a place offering shelter against the tropical showers that come down in the middle of the night: under a Jeep tied down on a wooden pallet, its wooden platform high enough to keep the rain from washing me down the deck.

Sometimes I wake and wonder what in hell I'm doing here. It's unreal. I'm safe and sheltered, but there's an agonizing knot in the pit of my stomach, a burl of guilt in my head. I'm twenty-five years old. Why should I be on this ship, so close to a battle getting fiercer by the day? Am I being fattened up now to die in the next few weeks, or am I to be spared—for what? I haven't even begun to live, and these are important questions. I think about the eighteen- and nineteen-year-olds dying on the island—in my place. Had they even a chance to ask such questions?

Army and Marine casualties at Peleliu are estimated at 2,000 dead, and 8,000 wounded and missing. All but a handful of the 10,700 Japanese die in the fighting.

We get reports of the cost of the slow, agonizing drive by the Division up the length of Peleliu. Scuttlebutt—the gossip passed along the Marine grapevine—had it that the three Marine regiments suffered losses of sixty-five percent or more: five of every seven Marines had been either killed or wounded.

But, unknown to us, we serve a purpose on the ship. We're out there in Kossol Passage, with many sub chasers and destroyers scurrying around us in plain sight of the Japanese, as a threat. The enemy generals are supposed to think that we, and several other troop ships, are a force ready to invade Babelthuap. Twenty-five thousand Japanese soldiers are held ready for this invasion, and therefore kept from supplying replacements on Peleliu.

Finally, when steak, potatoes, and ice cream are served to us one late afternoon as the *Sea Runner* makes its way back to Peleliu, we know what the next dawn will bring. It is D-18, eighteen days after the initial landing. In the murky morning, I climb down a net directly onto an LST, clinging frantically to the net with one hand while my heavy backpack pulls me down. My rifle swings against my helmet as my feet feel for rungs and the solid deck.

The LST moves sluggishly. It plows over a reef onto a coral slab on Purple Beach and lowers its bow, like a drawbridge over a moat. Our company, some three hundred of us, shuffle onto the island between rows of bearded, bedraggled Marines sitting along the sides of the road, waiting to embark on the landing ship.

I catch the eye of one, his unshaven face drawn and dirty, green fatigues torn and stiff with dust and mud. It takes all my willpower to keep from holding my nose. These men stink—of sweat, of vomit and piss, of caked blood and the guts of their buddies.

The whole island stinks. The stench hits me like a wall. I can't pinch my nostrils to mask the stink of death, of putrefying flesh, the foul odor of excrement strewn about wherever the battlefield has been, the sharp ammoniac smell of urine everywhere.

Half the island is overrun by thousands of Marines, infantrymen and tank crews, and bodies by the hundreds—mostly Japanese—mark their progress. One body we pass is maggot-infested under swarms of flies in the sweltering heat of day. At night, I'm told, the bodies are eaten by rats, some grown fat as cats.

Later I try digging into the coral with my small pickaxe. It's like chipping away at a cement road. No one is able to dig a hole either to bury a body or to shit into. It's easier to pass the body by. And to shit into your helmet and toss the dreck about.

I feel like a raw recruit again under the eyes of the weary veterans sitting on their downturned helmets. I wave a version of a salute as I shuffle past them. Some return the wave; others sit there, unseeing, dazed. They look like old men, these eighteen- and nineteen-year-olds, what's left of them.

The amphibious commanders are given bad intelligence on Peleliu's terrain. 'Aerial photos were defective,' naval historian Samuel Eliot Morison says, 'owing to cloud cover, heavy jungle growth and clever Japanese camouflage, which gave the general impression that this rugged island was low and flat.'

We march down a road broad enough to accommodate two trucks and foot traffic, kicking up chalk dust with every shuffling step. I walk beside Mickey, whose face runs with rivulets of sweat. My green fatigues are dripping wet under the blazing sun above and the heat of the coral at my feet. We come to heaps of battered cement buildings on the edge of a swamp. It's a clearing surrounded by a moonscape of the twisted remnants of palm trees, blackened ground smelling of death, big coral craters choked with shattered tree trunks, smashed tanks, battered helmets, scraps of boots, pieces of clothing.

The road stops at a row of tents, their ends open for whatever breeze can come through. I'm assigned to a tent with twelve cots, cramped six to a row. I dump my knapsack, relieved to be rid of the load, grab my rifle and line up with my platoon in front of the tents. We landed without hearing a shot, without firing a shot.

Mickey's next to me, Bruce in front, Martin and Ike in back. They're my buddies. We're at ease, waiting for the lieutenant's instructions.

Mickey points to the hills directly in front of us, a couple of hundred feet beyond the clearing. "Look at those hills. How in hell is anybody going to get up to the ridge?" he asks. The hills are pocked, craggy, steep, and, from what we're told, pitted with caves. "I hope we don't have to do it," Bruce says. He's a corporal with battle experience in Guadalcanal—one of the few veterans in our company. We always listen to him.

Our job, the lieutenant says, is to patrol the area between the swamp and the hills. A twenty-four hour watch is to be maintained. Each of us will take a four-hour watch (out of every twenty-four) to guard against Japanese infiltrators. I draw the midnight-to-four shift.

Several other companies of Marines and Army reserves are attacking the hills and caves. The enemy is able to push mortars out of the caves, fire them and draw them back in, toss grenades down the slopes, or snipe at patrols. They can't be seen. At night they come out of the caves and fire mortars and throw grenades into Marine lines. We learned later that the Japanese had honeycombed the coral hills with miles of tunnels. They'd enslaved the men and women of Angaur, a tiny island ten miles to the south, to dig the tunnels and huge caves that served as storage areas for food and ammunition, and as barracks, hospitals and communication centers. There was enough food stored to feed a division for an entire year.

SOMEONE GIVES ME a punch at 23:30 that first night. He jabs his rifle butt at the bottom of my feet hanging over the edge of my cot and hisses, "Okay, Mel. You're on. Get your ass going." I roll out of the cot, fully dressed, fumble into my shoes, shuffle to the mess tent with my rifle and helmet, sip a cup of bitter coffee, and accustom my eyes to darkness. The corporal of the guard leads me to my post at the north end of the clearing along the edge of the swamp.

I squat with my rifle in the crook of my arm and look into the shadows, listening to the whisper of insects in the mangrove. There's no moon, but some stars shine, and in a moment or two I make out shapes of tree trunks in the dim light. I stand up every ten minutes or so, or sit back on my haunches to avoid cramping. Time passes slowly.

After two hours, the corporal noisily returns to the post. "Password," I demand.

"World Series," he responds.

"You sure made a lot of noise," I say.

"Hell, yes. I wanted you to know I was comin'. I didn't want you to take me for a Jap."

He's lean and short; I can see his point. "I knew it was you," I said. "No Jap would've made so much noise." He laughs.

"Don't fall asleep," he warns, and disappears silently in the darkness.

I strain to make sense of the rustling, the muted hissing, in the swamp. Snakes? Japs slithering along the ground? I can see nothing. I hunch down and inch forward. In the dimness I glimpse a blob on the ground fifteen or twenty feet before me. It moves. My heart pounds. The blob moves again. It's too small to be a Jap. But I've never seen a Jap, except a dead one.

I raise my M-1, click off the safety catch and sight down the shaking barrel. My finger grips the trigger. My mouth goes dry. My stomach aches. The blob moves again, closer to my sight. I lower the rifle. It's a rat, and it *is* big as a cat. I bend down, pick up a piece of coral and throw a strike. I grip my rifle and sink down on the wet coral. I was afraid of a rat. What if it was a Jap? As dawn drifts in, the corporal of the guard noisily brings my relief.

I tell Bruce my story that morning in the mess tent. "It's a good thing you didn't shoot the varmint," he says. "You'd have woken the whole company. And they're so trigger-happy they'd shoot each other, maybe."

FOR A FEW WEEKS, it was four hours on guard duty and twenty off. The twenty went fast: eight hours for sleep, two for eating and ten for good works such as washing myself and my clothes using my helmet as a bucket, then joining squads of combat Marines resting from assaulting the nearby hills.

With Mickey, I'd edge up to the foothills leading to the ridges and hollows where the Japs were dug in. We avoided the artillery units firing barrages of shells into the scarred hills and blackened cave-mouths. The howitzers were the particular targets of Jap mortar shells. Nor did I venture out with patrols probing the hills, seeking out the gun emplacements. I wasn't *gung ho*. I didn't want to get killed. I just wanted to see what was going on, the reporter in me still working.

On one such innocent stroll with Mickey we were pressed into service as litter bearers. I heard, "Hey, you! Hey, Gyrene" coming from a huddle of green-clad forms just off the road. They waved to us. "C'mere. C'mere, for Christ'sake. Give us a hand." We stood a moment for a long look. We'd heard that Japs sometimes used such tricks.

But these were two worn and spent Marines, splayed out on the coral with an unconscious Marine on a litter between them. They'd carried the wounded kid—an unshaven eighteen-year-old—for hundreds of yards, finally giving in to the weight and the heat. Mickey didn't hesitate once he saw what was needed. He picked up one end of the litter, motioned for me to pick up the other, and we stepped off to the road towards the field hospital. The two Marines trotted beside us, one of them muttering "Where in hell is a fuckin' Jeep when you need one?" like a civilian wishing for a taxi on a rainy night.

They commandeered a Jeep coming toward us on the road. We lifted the litter crossways onto it and watched the men steady their wounded buddy while they trotted alongside. Their dungarees dripped, as if they'd showered in them. Their hands and eyes were on the litter, their burden, worry stamped on their faces. They weren't about to lose a buddy, a hard-to-come-by buddy, a brother conceived in boot camp, gestated in months of drills and dry runs, and born out of the loins of bloody battle.

Mickey and I observed this tableau and looked at each other with greater appreciation. We were buddies. We enjoyed each other. We looked out for each other. We stuck together against the lieutenant, the Marine Corps, the world.

We watched the Jeep bouncing slowly down the road. "I hope the kid makes it," I said to Mickey.

We walked back up the road to an area named The Horseshoe, a valley between cliff-like Bloody Nose Ridge and snarled, craggy Walt Ridge, where Marine Wildcats, taking off from the reconstructed airfield, dropped five-hundred-pound jellied gasoline bombs, burning off the remnants of trees and vines, trying to flush enemy soldiers out of their caves.

We sat on the ground, taking cover behind a wrecked and abandoned tank, looking at the flames as they smothered the hillside. Blackened holes—the caves—appeared in the ridges as the flames fanned out.

I watched a lone, scrawny Marine crawl up the sides of the ridge to one such cave. He carried a flame-thrower on his back, the apparatus appearing bigger and heavier than he. He inched his way up, a perfect target for enemy snipers on the ridge. One bullet on his flame-thrower and he would have been blasted skyward. But he made it, sprawling in front of the cave, directing shafts of flame deep into the hole.

A ball of flame spurted out of the cave, screaming, stumbling and rolling down the hillside, blackening the coral until it came to rest in the road, a charred, smoking, curled fetus.

"Jeezus," I mumbled. "The poor bastard."

Mickey shook his head. "Yeah, even if he is a Jap."

"Let's get the hell out of here." I felt a sudden fury. "This is fuckin' butchery!"

Mickey looked at me in disbelief. "Hey, buddy. What the fuck do you think this is? Hollywood? This ain't a movie. This is the real thing." He pulled away from the tank and stood up, removing his helmet to wipe his brow. His black hair, bedraggled and sweaty, glistened in the sun.

I was on the ground next to the tank, looking up at Mickey.

I heard nothing at first. I saw it: I saw a bullet hit him in back of the head. The sniper had aimed his sights on the tank and waited for one of us to come into his line of fire.

And then I heard it, a second later...the dull *thunk*. I sucked back the rising bile in my stomach as I watched Mickey's head slump. Eyes black and staring. Face suddenly ashen. Cheeks sagging. Streams of blood bursting from his nostrils as he leaned toward me, knees buckling, body falling, the coral turning red.

I scrambled to him. Kneeled over him. I couldn't help him. I couldn't breathe new life into him. I was too late to put my head between him and the sniper. All I could do was cry over him.

I WAS ON THAT ISLAND fourteen more months. There wasn't a day or a night that I didn't think of Mickey. To this day I think of him.

"This ain't a movie," he said. In the movies, the John Waynes and Ronald Reagans strutted on fake islands in fake battles; they picked themselves up in one piece and collected their paychecks.

You couldn't pick yourself up, wash the ketchup off your face and shirt and pants, give me that big grin of yours, slap me on the back and say, "C'mon, let's forget this shit," and pull out the chess set.

How quickly, how brutally your life was blown out, Mick. And two thousand other Marines on that stinking island.

It is questionable whether the advantages gained offset the terrible cost.

What "advantages"? Two days before the scheduled landing, Admiral "Bull" Halsey sent a dispatch to Admiral Chester Nimitz, Commander of all Pacific forces, urging the immediate cancellation of the Peleliu invasion. He recommended bypassing the Palaus, neutralizing the Japanese forces with air strikes, and speeding up the attack on the Philippines.

Nimitz didn't fully accept Halsey's advice. Commitments were already made for the attack on Peleliu, Nimitz replied. It "must go through as planned." Maybe Nimitz felt as General Rupertus did: the Japanese garrison was an easy mark—why worry?

What would have happened if Nimitz and the Joint Chiefs had adopted Halsey's suggestions? Mickey and two thousand Marine and Army troops might have been spared their deaths; 8,091 spared their injuries; the Japanese would have rotted in their caves and withered on their islands; MacArthur would have waded ashore ahead of schedule in the Philippines, Peleliu's feared airfield destroyed by Navy bombardment, not needing to be captured by the Marines.

I went through the motions of living from day to day on Peleliu. I was given a job as a clerk-typist in the Officer Messenger Mail Service, which handled super-secret documents the Navy didn't trust to the airwaves or telephone. Officers came at all hours to receive their sealed orders. I found it ironic that I was empowered to handle vital secrets.

And I pondered and discussed the vagaries of war with Bruce and Martin.

One night, Bruce managed to cadge a bottle of bourbon from a young Navy ensign who didn't drink. With Martin, we passed the bottle from hand to hand on Purple Beach. And we talked…about Chesty Puller, the vaunted Marine Colonel, who sent wave after wave of his men against the Japs at Bloody Nose Ridge only to see them shot down as fast as they attacked. "He's a Goddamned hero," Bruce said, waving the bottle aloft. "A true Marine."

Martin, a Navy corpsman who wanted to a doctor, grabbed the bottle from Bruce. "Puller's a butcher," he shouted on the deserted beach. "He's a fuckin' killer." Bruce tugged the bourbon from Martin's hand. "They're all killers," Martin screamed. "That's how they win." We had our most lucid moments on drunken nights.

Many days I hiked out to the Horseshoe and sat by the side of the road for an hour or two, hunched over my M-1, searching Walt Ridge for snipers. Some were still being flushed out of the caves, while the hunt for Japanese units in the ridges had long moved to other sectors to the north.

But as a Jew sitting *shivah* for a buddy, I still looked for the sniper who got Mickey.

Overshadowed by events in Europe and the Philippines, deprived of the publicity that made Guadalcanal, Tarawa and Iwo Jima household names, it became in the words of one historian, 'the forgotten battle.'

The "forgotten battle" finally ended when the Japs surrendered, eight months after September 15.

I can't forget. I will not ever forget.

I WALKED DOWN New York's Fifth Avenue in February, 1946, with my shipboard buddy, Sgt. Eddie Hanrahan. We'd been thrown together for thirty days on the LSD (Landing Ship, Dock) that carried us from Peleliu to San Diego. I had $600 in back pay. He had $900. We put up in a fancy hotel and blew it all in a month.

I was trying to forget Mickey, Peleliu and the letter I'd received from Dixie Lou. I was also waiting for her to return from France, where she'd gone as a dancer in a USO troupe. I was hoping against hope that she'd change her mind and welcome me back. Eddie was trying to forget that he had two more years to go on his enlistment; he was sick of the Marine Corps and the six years he'd spent in it.

I don't think we were too slobbering drunk that month. At least the manager of the St. Regis didn't throw us out. We had a good time in the dark, ritzy bars, trying to pick up the women we saw there. They'd eye us in our beribboned green uniforms and offer to buy us drinks.

We tried to drown reality, but it didn't work. And when Dixie Lou came back and I met her on a windy street corner, she dressed in a tight-fitting GI raincoat, her red hair whipping around her pinched face, I knew the messages of love she'd written about in 900 letters were just empty words.

Eddie began waking up in our hotel room screaming about giant flies buzzing around him, flailing out at them, whacking at them with pillows, bedsheets, and shoes. I hustled him into a cab that took us to a Naval hospital in Queens. The doctors there said he had the D.T.'s. I shook his hand as he sat in a wheelchair, but he didn't know me. I neither saw nor heard from Eddie again.

But he sobered me up. I began to try to pick up the life that had been sidetracked by my thousand days in the Marines.

I went back to the labor movement.

9

OAK RIDGE

I enlisted in the Southern Organizing Drive of the Congress of Industrial Organizations, the CIO, in the summer of 1946, and was assigned to the campaign in Oak Ridge, Tennessee—the city created to build the atomic bomb. Twenty thousand workers were employed there in three sprawling plants near the giant TVA power turbines on the Tennessee River. I was one of six battle-tested vets; the head organizer was a veteran unionist.

Charles Dannenberg, the 56-year-old president of a chemical factory union in Greenville, North Carolina, was in charge of the campaign. Second in command was Lou Krainock, a former Marine captain and an organizer for the Packinghouse Workers in Chicago.

Krainock stood over our group, seated on hard chairs around him in the CIO's council headquarters on the top floor of a downtown office building in Knoxville, twenty miles north of Oak Ridge. "Whadya say we introduce ourselves?" He smiled disarmingly. "If there are no objections, I'll start." He gazed at each man. There were no objections.

"See this hand?" he said. "I lost that middle finger on Tarawa. A Jap bullet busted the carbine I was holding." He paused, swallowed, and waved his right hand. "That bullet whizzed past my head, missed me by an inch. I'm lucky to be standing here." I shifted uncomfortably in my chair. Lou noticed and looked at me. "I'm an old union man. My pappy was a union man. The union made us strong. It makes all working people strong. That's why I'm here. That's enough speech-making for me." He dragged a chair over and sat facing the group.

Alvin, a six-footer, barrel-chested and broad-beamed, stood up next to Lou. "I'm an old union man, too," he said. "Used to be shop steward in Alcoa, up the river from here. I put in three years on Navy cans. Gunner. Came out nary a scratch." He glanced around the room, as if wondering what to say next. He scratched his rump. "I guess I'd ruther be an organizer than go back to that fuckin' mill." The men roared.

Dannenberg held up his hand. "Organizing ain't easy. There'll be some days when you'll want to get back to Alcoa," he said, dampening the laughter. "Okay, let's get on with it."

Bill stood, his hands clasped in back in the at-ease position. He was clean-cut, good-looking and graceful. The girls must go for him, I thought, as I watched him look assuredly around the room. He smiled, his teeth white and even. "I started work at Ford in Memphis when I was eighteen, and I found out right away that the union was my only protection. I got a chance to make the union bigger and stronger. That's why I'm here." He glanced at Alvin. "I was in the Navy like Alvin. Coxswain on Higgins boats. I took guys like Lou in. So I know how it was." He sat down.

Jake, gaunt and stooped, held onto the back of the chair. "Ah lied and got my fust job as a bobbin boy when ah wuz fo-teen. Ah thought ah'd never get out of that job nor Gastonia. But the Ahmy got me. Ah got to see the world. From the ground up." Lou snickered. "Yeah, ah crawled." He moved his elbows as if digging them into the ground. "Ah crawled up the beach and half-way 'cross France. I got froze in Bastogne." He smiled wryly. "Fust time ah ever seen so much snow. Cold snow. Freeze your ball bottoms off." He grinned. "But ah defrosted 'em. Ah'm here, like Lou. 'N ah'm a union man from when I was this high." He held his palm across his chest and sat back in his chair. Some of the men clapped. Everyone looked at me—the last one.

I reeled off my background as a reporter on West Virginia's *Welch Daily News*, editor of the *Voice of Labor* in Cumberland, Maryland and present editor of the monthly newspaper of the United Gas, Coke and Chemical Workers Union. "After being a Marine like Lou in the Pacific," I said, "I feel as lucky as he does. I didn't think I'd come out of it alive."

Dannenberg rose and cleared his throat noisily. "You've been hand-picked because you're dammed good union men and dammed good patriots," he said with the fervor of a country preacher. "No one, especially the AF of L, can question your patriotism. They wouldn't dare call you a damned Communist. They can't say you're trying to over-throw the government." He ran a broad, thick hand through his wavy black hair, and held it to his head for a moment, as if pondering his next statement. "We're here only to make sure the workers of Oak Ridge enjoy the fruits of their labor. We're here to spread the word of unionism…to unify the powerless worker…to help them compete on equal terms with Du Pont, Monsanto and Union Carbide." He glanced around the room at us, slumped over on hard chairs in a loose circle about him. "We're not fighting the government. We're fighting Du Pont, and the others—they're making millions and paying their workers pennies…."

Squirming in his chair, Lou said, "Hey, Charlie. What's your plan? How we goin' to organize this town?" He coughed into a fist that exposed the gap in his hand.

"Hold your water, Lou," Dannenberg said sharply, "I'm getting to that. But first I gotta tell you what the AF of L is doing. Those labor fakers are blasting away at *us*…not the companies. They're screaming that we're a bunch of Communists going to sell out the workers to Russia. They're telling the workers to join the AF of L because they're safe and have good labor relations with the big companies. Of course they do. They're miserable ass-kissers. We gotta expose 'em." He lowered his head and, under bushy eyebrows, glared at us. "They're the ones selling out…to the companies."

Lou coughed again. "Okay, Charlie. But what do we do? We're only five organizers. Six," he added hastily, looking at me. "Do we concentrate on one plant? Two? How long we got? Let's get down to basics. How about it?"

Charlie looked at Lou. His lips tightened, his jaw muscles twitched. He stood silently for a moment. "Okay, Lou. No more speeches." He sat on the edge of a desk and hunched over. "We're going to live out there…in the barracks. We got four months before the election. We're going to eat, sleep and shit with these people…and they're going to accept us…and trust us. We're going after Union Carbide. They're the worst. The rest will follow." He ran his hand through his hair.

OAK RIDGE was a military base and a Wild West town rolled into one. The two-story barracks, split into single cells and double rooms, their bathrooms at the ends of long hallways, were the typical buildings found on bases hastily built during the war. Row on row of these barracks were lined up along narrow dirt roads laced with poles and drooping wires. Board sidewalks led from the raw red clay roadway through muddy terraces up to each barrack.

Each of three factories refined plutonium and other bomb ingredients in separate processes; no one knew which would work. Their buildings stood windowless, prison-like in the treeless terrain bulldozed out of a long, lush hollow near the dams and hydroelectric plants of the Tennessee Valley.

We moved into the barracks, two to a room to save money. I was thrown in with Alvin, the Navy gunner and former aluminum worker. His face was chiseled, nose sharp, lips thin, chin square, eyes deep-set and blue, not coal-black, as I'd first thought. He had the beginning of a beer belly hanging over his belt. He seemed always to have a cigarette either in hand or hanging from his lips, his eyes crinkled against the smoke. I was alarmed to find that he often went to sleep with a burning butt in his mouth—especially after drinking heavily, which he did almost every night. It was all in the line of duty, Alvin said. You go where the workers hang out.

Television did not exist, and in a new town like Oak Ridge where even the churches had no everyday social programs, where there were no government- or company-sponsored lectures or concerts or dances, where the nearest movie was in Knoxville, the workers congregated in roadhouses, honky tonks, and saloons that lined the roads outside the atomic reservation or in Kingston and Lenoir City. Alvin and the others visited every bar every night to drink and talk to the men—and to the women.

I was wrapped around my typewriter, composing leaflets, brochures, pamphlets, newspapers, radio programs, newspaper ads and letters aimed at typical Oak Ridge workers. I hadn't met as many as Alvin, and I always asked him about their lives.

"Jeez," he said. "I can't figure out what they do. They're either scared about talking or they're very honest. Most of them say they just look at gauges and turn valves...all day and night long...turn valves. As far as I can tell, they don't know what in hell they're doing...and they didn't know what they were making until the bomb went off." Stretched out fully-clothed in the double bed we shared, he'd shake his head, puff on the cigarette held in his lips, cross his legs, and pass out. I'd extricate the cigarette, climb into bed and pull a blanket over both of us.

After a few weeks, our union hall attracted a dozen or more workers every evening, and maybe a hundred when plant meetings were advertised. The hall, two adjoining rooms in one of the barracks, was furnished with rows of folding chairs, sad-looking Salvation Army couches, a coffee pot and cookies on a table near a sink, a table for literature, and some desks for me and the organizers. It filled a need for many of the workers: a place to meet others, to talk, tell stories, joke and plan. Many of the people Alvin and the other organizers met in the roadhouses came regularly.

Among them was Betty: tall and broad-hipped, her dark-rimmed glasses made her look like a Midwestern school teacher. She took to the union with the zeal of a convert. It was she who suggested I write a soap opera for the Knoxville radio station everyone listened to, a kind of Fibber McGee and Molly program that was so popular then. She outlined story lines and I pounded out the scripts. They all dealt with work at Union Carbide, the boring routine, the nagging, suspicious supervisors, the stultifying atmosphere, the deadening environment in the town, the lack of democracy, and the fresh winds of change that would come through the CIO.

In a few weeks, we had a number of volunteers, many of them Betty's co-workers, eager to become actors on our weekly fifteen-minute programs. Betty and I chose good readers and soon had a repertory company going, whose members spent night after night making suggestions to improve the script, rehearsing their lines, polishing their diction, and building a camaraderie they didn't find at work.

To counter the AF of L accusations that the CIO was Communist, I wrote a script in which the actors applauded numerous government services, such as the post office. "If the post office were in private hands, interested in profits only," I remember writing, "you'd be paying twenty-five cents to mail a letter, instead of two cents."

We were elated the night we finished that program; it had gone well; everyone felt good about their work and the message. We piled into my pre-war Ford and headed south toward the union hall in Oak Ridge. Dusk turned to night, and the stars emerged above the dark hills as I drove slowly along the two-lane highway.

Suddenly I felt a jolt in back of me. At the same time someone in the back seat screamed, "Oh, my God. There goes a wheel."

The car rocked from side to side. I jammed my foot on the brakes, but there was no pressure. I tried to hold the car steady in the middle of the deserted road. It settled slowly and bumped along on a brake drum. Out of the corner of my eye, I could see the loose wheel wobbling down the road ahead of the car. Gradually, I eased to the side of the road and scraped to a stop in a ditch. We emerged, shaken.

My mind whirled. How could a wheel come off? Suppose we'd been going faster? The car would've flipped over. We could've been hurt or killed. I hadn't noticed anything wrong with the wheel when I drove it from Washington…what could've gone wrong?

Betty, her face drained of color, almost sobbing, embraced Amy, the other woman in our radio cast, and both of them rocked back and forth. Tom muttered: "God…damn…dammn," and stooped to inspect the brake drum. Joe walked around in a stupor, shaking his head, mopping his face with a grimy handkerchief.

Two cars on their way to Oak Ridge stopped when they saw us standing in the road next to the car in the ditch and gave us a ride to the union hall. That night, all night, I tossed with dreams of twisted cars and bloody, broken bodies.

After a tow truck pulled the car to a garage the next morning, we found that the cotter pin holding the wheel to the axle was missing. The mechanic said that either the pin had broken, in which case a piece of it would be found in the wheel, or someone had removed the pin.

They never found a broken piece.

Betty was sure one of the AF of L organizers had removed the pin while the car was parked at the radio station.

"They knew we'd be there," she theorized. "After all, everyone in town listens to the CIO Show, including those lame brains."

I shrugged. "There's no proof. You can't accuse anyone without proof."

She whipped her glasses off and frowned at me. "Who else would do such a despicable thing?" she asked, her voice shrill and angry.

I shook my head, suddenly weary, and leaned back in my chair, another vision rising in my mind of a tumbling car and battered bodies. "Let's get a beer someplace…if you don't mind riding with me."

Betty knew of a quiet place, and we drove through the wooded hills to a two-story house beside the road near Kingston. The place was aflame with light; it buzzed with chatter, laughter, music. A long bar inside was two-deep with men in jeans and khaki shirts. Tables around the small dance square were crowded with laughing couples, and we found chairs on the long glassed-in porch. Far from the jukebox that wailed and swung out the hits of the war years, we sipped our beer and looked at the stars.

"What made you take a job here?" I asked.

"Good money. Much more than I could make in Ohio. Besides, they said it was a secret project and that I'd be helping the war effort."

I listened to Harry James in the background: *It's been a long, long time.*

"I guess it was better than joining the WACS," I suggested. "At least you've had a little freedom."

"Not much." She looked at me quizzically, wondering, perhaps, what she could tell me. "It was like being in the Army…Army discipline…Army food…Army regulations…The worst of it was not knowing what you were doing and not being able to talk to anyone, even the people you worked with. But I was glad to get away from my family…be on my own…see the world." She giggled, shrugged a shoulder and looked down at her beer bottle. Then she raised it and swallowed a long draught. "I never drank beer before I came here," she said.

"You're pretty good at it now."

"I'm pretty good at a lot of things I never did before," she said, raising the beer bottle. "Here's to new experiences." She clinked my bottle. It belled in my mind, reverberating in a memory of pre-war toasts with my wife who, after three years of loving letters, brushed me aside with a "Dear John" that made me want to bury myself on my island.

From the jukebox came the warm soprano of Doris Day on a sentimental journey. I sipped my beer, and my eyes met Betty's.

EVERY WEEK I produced a four-page newspaper with stories that put the CIO in the best light: the CIO's efforts to overcome the wartime wage freeze, to tax the greedy war profiteers, to hold price controls on food and rents, and to obtain dignity and strength in the workplace. I picked up stories from the CIO News, but wrote features about our Oak Ridge organizers and their exploits as workers and veterans, each accompanied by a picture of the organizer, usually in his uniform.

To be reprinted in the paper, the photograph had to be converted to an engraving. The image was etched on metal so that it could be combined with the metal type of the stories run on a printing press. In Knoxville only one union shop made such engravings, and that's where I took my photographs. The AF of L took their work there, too.

Lou Krainock had written home for a large professional photo to accompany the story I wrote one week. It showed him resplendent in his officers' dress blues, campaign ribbons, Purple Heart and Bronze Star pinned to his chest—a handsome, rugged John Wayne type. Actually, he'd changed considerably since the photo; deep worry lines now creased his forehead, his eyes were puffy, the lightness and laughter in his eyes had dulled. But this photo, even though it was to be reduced, showed him at his best. I took it to the engraver in the morning, on my way to the print shop, where I was to make up the paper.

An anteroom off the stairs on the second floor of a large sunny loft led to the engravers' shop. Two benches and a table stood against the wall, near a small window that looked into the shop. There, one could view large cameras, racks of zinc and copper, and tanks of acid bath. I placed my brown envelope next to the window so that it could be seen. Within a few minutes, a shop worker stalked through a door to the anteroom for the envelope. As soon as the engraving was completed, it went back into the envelope and was stacked on the long table with all other finished work, ready to be picked up.

Later that afternoon, as I riffled through the envelopes for mine, I found a bulky one labeled *AFL*. There was no one in the room, so I pulled away from the window into a corner to check the AFL's engravings.

The envelope contained a photo of Charlie Doyle, vice-president of the Gas, Coke and Chemical Workers Union, and what purported to be his membership card in the Communist Party. Under Doyle's photo were numbers across his chest. It was a photo taken by the U.S. Department of Immigration and Naturalization, which had detained him at the border when he returned home from Canada. It made him look like a criminal.

It took me a minute to realize the AF of L planned a big anti-Communist campaign and that Charlie was going to be its whipping boy. It took me another second to recognize that the AF of L was getting help from government agencies, which claimed to be neutral.

I hurriedly stuffed the originals and engravings back into the envelope and stuck it under the pile on the table. What should I do?

The best thing was to take the envelope and walk out of there. But suppose I were caught? I'd be accused of thievery. How would that look? Nobody's going to catch you, I thought. Take it.

But I'd never stolen anything in my life. I just couldn't.

I sat on a bench in the room for ten minutes or so, wrestling with my conscience. No one came up the stairs; no one looked through the window from the shop. But I couldn't bring myself to take the envelope.

I returned to the print shop, sickened by the realization that our union's drive was to be derailed by vicious lies. After checking the final proofs of my paper, I watched it go to press. I made arrangements to return in the morning to pick up bundles that our organizers would hand out at plant gates.

As I headed back to Oak Ridge, I stopped at the engravers' again, took the stairs two at a time and rummaged through the envelopes on the table. The AFL envelope was gone; I was too late. For days afterwards, I berated myself.

Lou become a celebrity in Oak Ridge as a result of my story on his life. Previously, at the union hall, he was often the center of jokes about his missing finger. There were wisecracks, with sexual undertones, about how he'd lost the finger. I'd see him wince but turn away to hide his anger. That stopped now that everyone knew he'd had the finger shattered by a Japanese bullet.

Our organizers didn't make him the butt of their jokes; he'd won their respect and admiration by being principled and adamant enough to force Dannenberg to change a bad decision.

ONE MORNING, over doughnuts and coffee with the organizers, Dannenberg announced that Negro workers would be asked to attend separate meetings. Lou coughed nervously.

"What's your reason for this, Charlie?" he asked.

"Why, we're in the South, Lou. They don't allow the mingling of races anywhere—the schools, buses, trains, restaurants. You know that." He lifted his hand to his hair, patting the waves. "Much as I hate to do it, we got to concur. That's been my policy all this time I've been organizing in North Carolina—and it's been successful. We can't organize by antagonizing the whites."

"Bullshit," Lou roared, crouching as if ready to attack. "Most of the people here aren't from the South. They couldn't care less about Southern customs, especially the hateful ones. Besides…besides, they've been working side by side with Negroes since these damned plants opened."

"Lou's right," Alvin said.

"Wait a minute, Al," Lou said. "Let me finish." He turned to Dannenberg.

"We got a policy in the CIO of no discrimination…in auto…in steel…in the packing houses in Chicago where I come from. How do you suppose we organized those shops? Separate white and separate black? Hell, no."

"This ain't Chicago, Lou," Dannenberg said, his face flushed. "Goddammit, this is the South…the fuckin' lynch mob South."

"We'll never get anyplace…especially in the South…if we give in to the lynch mob and its mentality," Lou said, glaring at Dannenberg.

"Charlie, let me as' you a question," asked Jake, the thin, lank-haired fabric inspector from Gastonia, in his high-pitched voice. Everyone laughed. Jake grinned, enjoying the laughter. "Did you talk to any of the Nee…gro workers or did you dee…cide this on your own?"

Dannenberg squirmed. "On…on my own."

"Dammit," Lou stormed. "Then you've violated CIO policy…and principles. You're wrong. Everyone here says so." He looked at the men around him. They nodded. "We can't do what the AF of L is doing. They've got two separate unions…neither of them worth a hill of beans." His voice softened. "Charlie. You've got to drop this idea. It hurts our campaign."

Dannenberg shifted uneasily in his chair. "I just thought I'd test the idea on you all first." He swallowed nervously a few times. "Okay, let's get together first thing tomorrow."

I went back to my Underwood to peck out another script, but mainly to hide. I was ashamed of Dannenberg and myself, he for his misguided policy, me for not speaking up like Lou. The others picked up literature, mapped their door-to-door canvassing of barracks or leafleting at plant gates, and left the hall. Dannenberg stared glumly at the wall.

AT DUSK, AFTER WORK, I clattered along the boardwalk to our bachelor quarters. I wanted to have a beer with the guys and talk. I knocked on Lou's door. No answer. I knocked on Bill and Jake's door. All three were there, already sharing beer and stories. They agreed to meet in the lobby while I went to get Alvin. I heard them noisily navigating down the hallway and stairs to the lobby. Their raucous laughter stopped abruptly, then I heard angry shouts and shrieked obscenities.

I ran down the hall and stairs and saw four burly men facing my three friends. One of the four, whose face I couldn't see, towered over Lou and was taunting him: "Okay, you fuckin' hero. You're going to lose more than a finger." He shuffled toward Lou. "You're going to lose your fuckin' head…and your balls…you CIO cocksucker."

Without thinking, I jumped on the tough, slammed my knee into his back as I'd been taught in the Marine Corps and shoved him into the wall. He fell to his knees and tried to get up. My knee hit his chin and drove him down again. He grunted and clung to the wall.

I heard the sounds of body blows, labored breathing, scuffling and scraping on the floor and I twisted, for a moment, to watch Lou, Bill, and Jake beating the three strongarms.

I turned back to mine. He dragged himself up and stood against the wall, shaking his head, scowling at me with bloodshot eyes. He raised his hands in a fighter's crouch and moved toward me. In one motion, I brought my knee to his groin, pushed my body against his chest and grabbed his throat with my right hand, ramming him against the wall. I squeezed his windpipe, beat his head against the wall and kneed his groin again and again.

I don't know for how long. Lost in rage, all I could think of was...holding my father by the throat...squeezing...Then I heard Lou saying: "Mel, Mel. For Godsakes, don't kill the bastard. Turn him loose."

I let go of my grip and the man gasped—loud, deep, sucking, gasps, then slipped down the wall. He sprawled on the floor, his chest heaving, his mouth biting at air.

Lou kicked his outstretched foot. "Why'd you jump us, you bastard?"

He crawled to his knees, lifted himself slowly to his feet, and stumbled out the door without a word.

When we finally crowded into a booth in a dark saloon, everyone agreed the men were AF of L goons.

"Never saw any of 'em before," Bill said in a slow drawl, rubbing his hands to ease his bruised knuckles. "They wuzn't after our money or nuthin'. They sure went after Lou." He clapped me on the shoulder. "I'm glad you jumped that bastard, Mel. They had us cornered but you busted 'em up."

I looked around. The tabletop was carved with hearts and arrows and initials and wet with beer suds and dripping bottles. The place smelled of beer and urine and sweat. Still bewildered by my impulsive action, I remembered, with a shudder, that time I was sixteen, shaking with fear, when I struck—tearful, blind, my arms like windmills…driving him away from my brother.

So I was still fighting him: the first tyrant in my life: my father. So I still carried it: that deep, terrible anger. Does it ever go away? Will it ever go away? Would this wipe the slate clean?

Sure enough, the AF of L splashed Charlie Doyle's picture and the forged Communist Party membership card on leaflets strewn about the three plants around Oak Ridge barracks. I hadn't told anyone about my inability to walk away with the AFL envelope at the engravers; I was ashamed to admit my weakness. Now I had to feign surprise at the AF of L attack and figure out counter-measures.

Betty and her co-workers were a big help. They attributed the assault on Charlie Doyle to AF of L's desperation in not dealing with issues that really troubled Oak Ridge workers.

"So what?" Betty argued in a meeting. "The Communists were with us in the war. And we won the war, didn't we?" Then, with a big grin, she said, "Maybe we need some real Communists here to get the companies to notice us!"

Our next radio show was called "The Red Herring Stinks."

When we left the radio station we checked the wheels and drove back to Oak Ridge, where we were met at the union hall by an agitated Dannenberg. His white shirt, usually starched and shiny, was wrinkled and sweat-stained, his hair tangled.

"I got subpoenaed today," he announced. "Some congressman is holding a hearing this Friday and I have to testify."

"What congressman?" I asked. "What for?"

"His name is Wood—John Wood…and the subpoena didn't say what for."

"There's got to be a purpose for a hearing…some legislative purpose."

Dannenberg shook his head. "We only have one week left before the election. It's got to do with that."

He was right.

WOOD, IT TURNED OUT, was a notorious racist from Georgia running around the country as chairman of the House Committee on Un-American Activities. It had launched a campaign against Communists in unions—especially unions of government workers.

The hearing room, on the second floor of the Knoxville Post Office, had one ceiling-high window through which the morning sun poured, glinting on polished oak chairs arranged in rows, reflecting off tables lining one side of the room. On the walls were framed engravings of George Washington, Robert E. Lee, and a photograph of President Harry S. Truman.

Seated behind the smaller tables were a half-dozen men dressed in rumpled suits, a few with collars loosened and ties hanging askew. They fingered notebooks before them: the press, I assumed. Dannenberg and I sat on chairs in the last row. His face was ashen, and he looked nervously and suspiciously at everyone.

The buzz of muted conversation stopped when a gangly, stoop-shouldered man shuffled into the room. A slick-haired man ran to his side, escorting him to a leather swivel chair behind the long table.

Looking about the room, his lips compressed, his chin outthrust as if to assert his authority, Congressman Wood announced: "This hearing of the Sub-committee on Communists in Unions is hereby called to order. And now, I'll turn the preliminary inquiry over to the chief investigator for this committee, Mr. Adamson."

Bulky and bull-necked, Adamson had been in the headlines recently for chasing alleged spies in Canada. He looked over his spectacles. "Thank you, Mr. Chairman," he intoned. "This committee has more than Communists in unions to be concerned with, Mr. Chairman. We have a serious and dangerous situation with regard to the scientists in the Oak Ridge atomic laboratories. It appears that there are subversive elements who are seeking to turn the laboratories over to a world government...maybe even a Communist government. Mr. Chairman this is an unthinkable situation. We must get to the bottom of it…we must prevent…"

Wood interrupted. "I agree, Mr. Adamson," he drawled. "I agree 100 percent. Now, we don't have too much time here today. I suggest, suh, that you call your first witness. Let's get on with it."

Adamson opened a folder, studied it for a moment, raised his head and mumbled angrily: "Joe Grotti. Is Joe Grotti here? Will he please step forward."

A short man, his ample bulk enclosed in a well-tailored blue suit, stepped up. Adamson swore him in perfunctorily and waved him to a chair on the other side of the table.

It turned out that Grotti was employed by the local utility in Buffalo and had been brought to Knoxville just to testify.

"Do you know of a man named Charles Doyle?" Adamson asked.

"Oh, yes," Grotti replied. "He's a Communist. Right now he's vice-president of the union at our company in Buffalo—the same ones trying to organize in Oak Ridge."

"How do you know he's a Communist?"

"I used to be in the union with him, and he was always talking about the working people taking power away from the bosses…stuff like that." Grotti leaned forward in his chair, as if to speak confidentially.

"Didn't you show me his Communist Party card?" Adamson prompted.

"Oh, yes, sir. Here's a copy of it," Grotti pushed a small card to Adamson.

"I enter this in the record, Mr. Chairman, as Exhibit 1," Adamson said. He turned to Grotti. "How did you get this?"

"Well, sir, in my job at the company I collect all kinds of information. Someone in the union gave it to me."

Adamson plodded along in his questioning until Wood said, "Mr. Adamson. 'Scuse me. I'd like to ask the witness whether he was aware of Mr. Doyle's arrest."

"Oh, yes, sir. It was in all the papers. I have…"

Wood held up a hand. "Tell me," he drawled, "was Doyle going into Canada to organize the scientists there in a Communist organization?"

Grotti stared at the Congressman for a moment. "Oh, yes…yes, sir. He was under orders to organize for the union. The president of the union said so himself."

I shivered. What Grotti was saying was that Marty Wagner, president of the union, ordered Charlie Doyle to cross the border into Canada. The Immigration Service waited for him to return and arrested him. Was it a setup? Wagner rid himself of a rival who was running for president against him; the company rid itself of a strong union man; the INS got its hooks on Doyle, who had come from Scotland as a young man and never became a citizen, and the Un-American Committee gained an explosive issue.

It was anticlimactic when Dannenberg was finally called to the witness chair. He denied that he or the union was Communist; he admitted that there could be some Communists in the union, just as there were some Communists in the country; as far as he was concerned, he never worried about Communists; he denied that Doyle had anything to do with the union's organizing policies in Oak Ridge; he denied that the union was attempting to establish itself in Oak Ridge as a means of obtaining atomic secrets.

"Mr. Dannenberg, why is your union organizing atomic workers, a small labor force in the South, when there are many other factories you could be organizing?" Adamson asked, slipping his specs down his nose to get a better look at Dannenberg slumped in the chair.

Wood bellowed. "Yes, Dannenberg. Why? I'll tell you why. Because you want those atomic secrets. You're nothin' but a dirty *spy*! Your union is a front for spies!"

I could see the reporters at the small tables scribbling in their notebooks. The chairman had given them some sensational quotes.

Dannenberg's hands came up to his chest as if to defend himself. He stared at Wood. "That's...that's not true." His voice quavered. "No. We're not spies. We're...we're as patriotic as you are...."

Wood banged his gavel. "Don't insult me. The whole CIO is a bunch of Reds and spies." His gavel hit the table again. "Next witness." Adamson smiled gratefully at his chairman, shuffled some papers, and said he had no further witnesses.

Dannenberg watched Wood and Adamson leave the room. His hands shook as he took a handkerchief from a coat pocket and wiped his brow. "Bastards, bastards," he muttered.

I patted his arm. "You did well," I assured him. "This wasn't a hearing. They weren't searching for truth."

Dannenberg nodded. "I know," he said wearily. "They wanted headlines and they want the AF of L to win. The bastards."

We went glumly back to Oak Ridge. Over a beer with Lou, I described the staging of the hearing and the obvious collusion of AFL and House Un-American Activities Committee. Lou shook his head sadly. "And we put our asses on the line for these miserable fakers."

The next morning the Knoxville and Memphis newspapers were full of amplified charges made by Wood and Adamson, quoted as saying that the CIO was cooperating with societies formed by Oak Ridge scientists wanting to place the atom bomb in the hands of a world organization. "These societies are definitely opposed to Army supervision at Oak Ridge," Adamson told the newspapers, "They're just waiting for the day when the military administration will be thrown out."

So the Army was in on the set-up, too. Maybe the AFL wasn't the only suspect in the sabotage of my car.

Local newspapers carried scare headlines for three days before the election. The AF of L reprinted the stories in leaflets that rained down over the reservation. Rather than add to the paper war, our organizers worked from morning far into the night knocking on doors, and standing at plant gates. I abandoned my desk and joined the others talking to workers one-on-one or in small groups. It was exhausting.

It was even more exhausting for me, because I kept berating myself for having givin the AFL and the Un-American Committee the opportunity to control the final few days of our drive. And because I couldn't tell anyone that I'd been too honest, too scared and too stupid to take that AFL envelope.

Only when the elections were over did I stop the self-flagellation.

The voting was heavy in two of the plants: Union Carbide, where workers voted overwhelmingly for the CIO, and DuPont, where the AFL squeaked through in a close vote. At Monsanto the small vote was in favor of no union, by a narrow margin; the CIO came in second.

Our organizers, except for Dannenberg, were elated with the results. Dannenberg believed we should have won them all, and in the next few weeks, I was told, he worried himself into a nervous breakdown.

Betty, thrilled with the election outcome, became one of the officers of the new local union. We corresponded after I returned to Washington—until I was fired by the CIO president himself.

Phil Murray had read a front-page story in the Pittsburgh *Press* about a woman who was granted a divorce by a Pittsburgh judge because she swore her husband had forced her to attend Communist meetings and, at times, had even left her alone at home in order to attend such meetings.

That husband was me, and I never forced Dixie Lou to do anything. The CIO president did not ask for my side of the story. "Communist" was all he saw and heard.

SURE, I WAS A COMMUNIST. I'd joined the Party in 1940, right after *The Argonauts* had been published. But I'd never attended any meetings, never had a chance to read the *Daily Worker*, and rarely saw any party literature. I didn't pay any dues because there wasn't anyone to pay dues *to*. I was a party member in limbo, so to speak.

When I took the CIO job, no one asked me whether I was a Communist. I didn't flaunt my beliefs, but I didn't hide them. That was probably the first instance of the Don't Ask, Don't Tell policy of the '90's.

After I was fired by the CIO, I hung around Washington and made up for lost time. I went to meetings, met many party members, scanned the *Worker* daily, caught up on my reading, and dated Diana Farnham, another redhead—but tall, willowy, beautiful, funny and smart.

I'd met Diana while working at the Gas, Coke and Chemical Union offices in a dilapidated building housing many other unions in the low-rent district on Fourteenth Street. One morning, as I rushed toward my office on the fourth floor, I caught a vision of a red-haired young woman in a white, summery dress, bent over a typewriter, clacking away with professional speed. I'd never seen her before, though I'd passed this office many times. *United Office & Professional Workers Union* was painted on the door.

I stopped short and conjured some excuse to interrupt her typing. "Hello," I mumbled. "I'm your next-door neighbor. My name is Mel. What's yours?"

She looked up. She smiled sweetly, knowingly. She'd heard this before. "Hello, neighbor," she said. "I'm pleased to meet you." She went back to her typing.

"Could I borrow a sharp pencil?" I fumbled. "Mine are all dull and I don't have a sharpener and I…"

"Sure," she said and stood up. She took my breath away. She was liltingly graceful, and in her clinging white dress, a choreography of light. I fell in love with her right there and then. She bent over a desk, rummaging. Her back was as enticing as her front. She picked up two pencils and presented them to me. "Are these okay?" she asked.

"Oh, yes," I said. "Perfect."

"My name is Diana," she said.

We went hiking along the towpaths of the old Potomac Canal, visited museums and the National Gallery of Art, attended meetings and lectures, drank and partied with Diana's friends on weekends, splurged occasionally by dining in inexpensive restaurants. We talked, argued, exchanged histories and views—finding comfort in each other. Who cared about unemployment and an empty wallet? We were in love.

When Diana's father came to town I met him at the Folger Library, where he was researching a book on Shakespeare. A slight man with a large, grey-thatched head, he was chairman of the English Department at the University of California at Berkeley and a noted Shakespearean scholar. Over lunch, I asked him for Diana's hand. He was surprised, and, I thought, charmed that he was being consulted about his daughter's well-being; he was wise enough to realize that she, not he, was making the decision.

He had more than a fatherly curiosity and questioned me about my boyhood, my parents, their background, my beliefs, my prospects, my concern for Diana. We talked for four hours; at the end, he shook my hand and pronounced his blessing: "May you both be very happy."

Diana, though she'd left home at eighteen to escape a stepmother—a belittling scold whom her father would not, or could not, challenge—was elated by her father's approval. We were married May 10, 1947, in a garden in Virginia before a host of friends and Diana's doting Aunt Minna and Uncle Paul.

On our honeymoon we took a train to Cumberland, Maryland, my pre-war home. I felt I belonged there, and decided to look for a job while Diana went back to her work as legislative representative and lobbyist for the United Office and Professional Workers Union. We saw each other on weekends, when Diana would ride the B & O to Cumberland, where I had a room in the Queen City Hotel, right over the station and next to the tracks.

Our meetings and lovemaking were accompanied by the hissing, chugging and rumbling of the big, coal-fired locomotives and the clacking rhythms of steel wheels on the rails. We didn't hear much of it; we were truly in love.

10

BEAD BOY

"**N**ow hiring," the ad in the Cumberland *News* said—an unusual notice, for Kelly-Springfield, one of the large factories in Western Maryland, rarely had openings; a job there was almost permanent. I needed an *almost* permanent job, anything to make more than the $20 a week unemployment insurance I was getting.

I gulped my coffee, left a nickel tip, paid my bill of twenty-five cents for the two doughnuts and coffee I'd consumed and left the Queen City Cafe to catch a bus to the tire factory. It was time for the seven-to-three shift change, and buses came every few minutes.

Half-filled with sleepy, disheveled men sprawled on the hard seats, the bus puttered down Main Street, stopping every two blocks for more rubber workers. Then it swung left on Mechanic Street to the five-story factory, its windows sooty, its bricks grimy with the dust of pulverized rubber. At the iron gates, I followed the line of workers through. I waited until the last man shuffled into a long hallway, where rows of timecards were strung along the wall. Off this hallway, I found the personnel office.

It wasn't quite seven o'clock, but five other men were already in the room: three young, like me, and two middle-aged. They were dressed in jeans and tee-shirts, appropriate for an August morning in 1946. I had on my green Marine fatigues. I was different, glad I hadn't gone back to my hotel room to change. Slumping against the wall, I waited and watched the room fill with men.

A young woman, her head and eyes down, came into the room and handed out applications and pencils to the men crowding each other. I sat on the floor and filled in the blanks. I stressed my Marine Corps service, gave as reference a gas station owner for whom I'd once done a favor, and forgot that I'd been to college, edited the *Voice of Labor,* or been publicity director of the CIO United Gas, Coke and Chemical Workers Union. I was the fifth man called.

The personnel man, stubby and chesty in a white shirt and knitted tie, looked me up and down. "How do you like the Queen City Hotel?" he asked. His head was like a block, squared off by a broad chin and blond brush of hair.

"It's noisy as hell. But it's clean. I'm only staying there until I find an apartment."

He nodded and smiled. "I stayed there one night. I thought the trains were coming through the room all night long." He studied my application.

"You don't have much experience in factories."

I shrugged. "The Marine Corps wasn't a factory. I couldn't…"

He broke in. "That's okay. I understand." He initialed a corner of the application. "Go through that door to the doctor's office. Then come back."

The doctor probed my chest and back with a stethoscope. "Ever had…" and he rattled off a list of ailments from a sheet on his desk. I shook my head to all of them.

"Pull your pants down."

I thought, Jeez, another short-arm inspection. He fooled me. He held my shorts and testicles and said, "Cough." I coughed. "Okay," he grunted and had me turn around slowly. "Any battles?" he asked.

"One," I said.

"No wounds. No scars. You came out of it in one piece."

"One piece," I echoed. The wounds were a lost buddy and a lost wife. "Okay, son," he said. "You're okay."

I WAS ASSIGNED as a bead boy to the second shift, three to eleven. I found out what a bead boy did when I reported for work that afternoon at 2:30.

He pushed a cart full of beads—circles of heavy wire, coated with something that looked like electrician's tape—to the fifty or so tire builders on the third floor. The beads came in three sizes, each size determining the diameter of the tire. They were the inner bases of tires formed at machines that looked like huge waffle makers.

I could only glimpse part of the process of tire-making as I pushed the cart around the floor, stopping at each waffle machine to fill the spokes on a nearby clothes-hanger-like stand, with beads numbered *14* or *15* or *16.*

I loaded one rack with 14's and saw a burly, muscular man, a grimy apron tied to his waist, fit a bead on top of a strip of burlap-looking material and thin sheets of rubber in the center of the machine.

While I pushed my cart to the next machine, I watched a hollow-cheeked man roll strips of thicker rubber around the inside of the waffler.

At the next rack down I saw another tire-maker roll more rubber strips to the top of the waffler and insert a second bead. As I made my way around the floor, I could see the hinged tops of the wafflers come down and clouds of hissing steam emerge, the machines baking and maturing the tires. The smell of burning rubber permeated the room.

I had to hustle to keep the racks full of beads. When my cart was nearly empty, I pushed it to the large freight elevator and to the first floor stockroom for another load.

A fully loaded cart full of *14's, 15's* and *16's* isn't easy to push around. I couldn't keep track of how many loaded carts I pushed and pulled around the floor that night—enough to make my shoulders ache. Glad to see the shift end, I settled heavily into the bus seat on my way to my hotel room.

THE ORNATE VICTORIAN-STYLE Queen City Hotel occupied the second and third floors of the Cumberland Railroad Station, a major stop on the B & O line. Every locomotive on the run between Washington, D.C. and Chicago stopped there for coal and water and to change crews. Engineers, firemen, conductors or brakemen who didn't live in Cumberland stayed at the hotel, lulled to sleep by the tolling bells, the snorting of engines starting their run, the short whistle-shrieks, and the constant squealing of brakes. The trains set the rhythm of the city, halting its traffic by straddling the main streets; the hissing and pounding of the straining locomotives, their punctuating bells and whistles, were its rock and roll.

That night I couldn't sleep. I heard every brake, bell, whistle and wheel. I pushed and pulled carts until daybreak, when the sun filtered through the dusty lace curtains on my windows overlooking the tracks. I'd worked up a big appetite; I washed my face quickly in the sink in a corner of the room and walked down one flight to the cafe next to the ticket office and waiting room.

"Mornin', Hazel." I watched her pour my coffee. "Lemme have a stack, lots of bacon and some home fries. And more coffee." I watched her slouch to the kitchen, her tight apron string tied in the back, accentuating an hourglass figure.

As I ate I described my new job to her.

"Don't sound like much," she said, and went off to attend to two more customers.

"It's a job," I muttered to the stringy bow fluttering on her back. It's better to have a job than to be unemployed. Unemployment can drive you crazy—make you feel worthless, unwanted, unneeded. It isn't good for the soul to mooch a handout—a lousy twenty bucks a week in the government's unemployment benefit program for veterans—the 52-20 Club.

Phil, the Party organizer in Baltimore, had suggested earlier that I occupy my time between unemployment handouts by acting as Party organizer in Western Maryland. "It'll keep you busy while you look for a job," he said.

Busy wasn't the word for it. Maddening was more like it. Getting people together for meetings: Cecil and Rick, who worked first shift, Earl and Harry and Nick on second shift, Boyd and Tom on third shift at Celanese, where they made fabric like nylon. There was only one shift at the laundry, but Beryl's husband at Celanese worked the swing, and you never knew when she could sit down to a meeting. Follow-up was hardest. Getting a tired textile worker, just off work, to follow through on writing a leaflet was like moving a mountain. To make sure something was accomplished, I gave up trying to move mountains and did it myself. That turned out to be worse: no one did anything; I did everything. An organizer in reverse.

"I quit, Phil," I said when I saw him at a meeting, a few days before hiring on at Kelly. "I'm not an organizer. And I don't want to be."

"No great loss," he said, wrinkling his lip. Not even a thank you.

I did like one aspect of the job of Party organizer, however. I was given a chance to visit the homes of Party members, meet their families, socialize with them, and observe their lives outside of meetings. Whenever I could, I'd wrangle an invitation to dinner or a Saturday breakfast. It was more than sociability or the need to get out of my little room that compelled me to seek the invitations. It was the curiosity of the reporter—the writer in me.

It was also the curiosity of a middle-class kid looking over the fence at real workers. Despite work in my father's print shop, and my work as a journalist and as a labor organizer, I had little first-hand knowledge of how the working class lived. I could read all of Marx's *Capital*, or all of the "proletarian" novels of the time and still have only a glimpse of the real thing. Now that I was trying to sink roots in this industrial city, I wanted to know the *how* and *what* of life as a worker.

One of my first visits was to Harry and Betty's bungalow, a short bus ride from the hotel. Harry, a spinner in the Celanese plant, had been a Party member for more than a year. I brought three bottles of beer as my contribution to the dinner. I couldn't afford any more. Betty, thin, pinched-face and withdrawn, busied herself at the kitchen stove. Harry, broad and hulky, drew me to the kitchen table and opened his beer. "Here's to the revolushon." He lifted his bottle and sucked down most of it. Betty dropped a pot lid and fled from the room.

Harry shrugged, finished off the beer and peered into the pots on the stove. "She's tetchy when I talk about revolushons." He grinned. "She's goin' to have to get used it. Right?" He placed three plates on the table. "Betty," he yelled. "Come on out here and serve us." Harry cocked an ear. "Betty. Get yer ass out here!" Silence. "Oh, shit," he said. "Fuck 'er—let's eat." He picked up the pot and spooned beans onto his plate and mine. "Betty," he shouted. "Fuck you. I'm drinking your beer." He piled two hot dogs on my plate. "Enough? You want more?" he asked. I shook my head. He put the rest on his plate. "Screw her, the bitch."

I looked at Harry. "Shut up and eat," I said.

Another night I visited Rick and Margery and their five children in their dank tar-papered house. Rick, also a spinner, had been an early union man and a Party member for several years. Margery, still youthful-looking with her long curled hair, shushed her three runny-nosed toddlers as she dished up bowls of cabbage and potatoes. I'd brought a small cake, and the children kept eyeing it while forking bits of food to their mouths. "We can't afford meat," Margery said apologetically as she piled potatoes on my plate. "These kids drink a lot of milk," Rick explained. I looked around at their meager furnishings and thought that working men like Rick could do nothing else to better their lives than dream and fight for a system that could lift them out of endless, grinding poverty.

Hazel was right. Being a bead boy was not an earth-shaker of a job, but at seventy-five cents an hour I earned $30 a week, far from what I'd made as editor, but still more than the 52-20 Club. I had enough for a few beers now and then after work, and could feel free to splurge by going out with the guys and their wives on weekends when Diana came up from Washington.

We hung out with George and Allie and Boyd and Evelyn. George was president of the Celanese local; Boyd vice-president. Both had worked in the spinning room at the plant for years before the war.

"My daddy was the first president of the Mine Workers in Lonaconing," George would say when he had a couple of beers in him and was feeling proud.

Tall and beefy, he had the shape of a pear. His chest had settled around his hips after years of standing eight hours a day before his charges—four noisy spinning machines. His hearing had been affected. But if he heard anyone even whisper any criticism of the labor movement, his belly moved up to his chest. "The UNION is the only protection the working man has," he'd bellow. "Remember that. The UNION puts us on the same level as the bosses!"

After the war and his discharge from the Army, he was elected union president. He had the uncommon ability of besting company managers in negotiations.

Boyd, bulky and moon-faced, hired on at Celanese right out of high school, and in a few days had mastered the spinning machines. "I used to watch those webs spin into the cones," he told me once over a few beers, "and I thought to myself, will I be doing this—tied to a machine—the rest of my life?" When the union came to the gates and handed out leaflets, Boyd knew instinctively that it was his way out.

ON THE JOB ONE NIGHT I tried to talk to some of the tire-makers as they pulled down the upper half of their waffle irons and waited for the machine to bake and steam the rubber into a tire. There was a little time for the tire maker to light a cigarette and talk.

"How long you been doing this?" I asked one while unloading my batch of beads.

"Too friggin long," he said softly as he took a last puff and ground the cigarette out with his blackened boot. In one motion, he stabbed his hand into a glove, raised the lid of his machine and dragged a still-steaming tire from it. "Too friggin long."

The next morning, Harry unexpectedly came to the hotel. "I'll buy you a beer, Mel," he said as we stood at the door to my room and he realized I wasn't about to invite him in.

"It's too dammed early for a beer," I said. "I'll have some breakfast." I followed him down the stairs to the cafe. His thick arms and shoulders were bunched under a skin-tight summer shirt; his arms hung loosely, but his hands were clenched in fists.

He chose a booth in a dark corner of the cafe and I watched him as he poured brew from a pitcher into his glass, his brow furrowing in concentration. Lifting his glass, he clinked my coffee cup: "To the revolushon."

I said nothing, staring at him, trying to figure him out.

Harry's chin was pointed, and his mouth kept moving like the mouth of a fish. His head, small for his big body, made him look unfinished.

"You know," Harry said, "you don't know me."

I took a long gulp of coffee.

"Comrades should know each other. Doncha think?"

I took another gulp. "What're you getting at, Harry?"

"Didja know I'm a di-rect descendant of one of the signers of the Declaration of Independence? Yessir. Di-Rect."

"I heard something about that, Harry, but I thought it was bullshit."

"No, sirree. Nothing doing. No bullshit. Di-Rect." He shook his head and grinned at me, his small teeth glinting with beer foam. "My great-great-great-great granddaddy was Josiah Bartlett. One of the or-i-ginal signers of the Declaration of Independence. Right under John Hancock. Josiah Bartlett. Yessirree." He downed what was left of his beer and waved to Hazel for another pitcher. He stared dumbly at the foam slipping over the sides of the pitcher. "Yessirree. Di-Rect."

"Whadya want me to say? Wow? Okay. Wow."

"Thas why I like revolushons. We'll kill the capitalists like my granddaddy killed the Redcoats. We'll kill the priests and the fuckin' politicians and the scumbag cops. And the judges. Oh, yeah, the judges. We'll clean 'em all out."

"Wait a minute, Harry. Who's talking about killing? Where'd you get that shit?"

"Revolushons means killings. Killings means revolushons. That's what I know."

"You didn't learn that from me. Or the Party. The Party advocates peaceful revolutions. People are going to *vote* to change the whole system. *Vote*, I said. Not kill."

"Revolushons means killings," he insisted, shaking his head like a pit bull gripping a throat.

"No it don't in this country. No one in this country will buy a bloody revolution. It's gonna be peaceful. They're going to vote for it."

"All I know is that in the revolushon we'll kill soldiers, cops, priests, anybody gets in the way. We'll take over the churches. Make 'em schools. Right? Take over the factories. We'll own 'em. Right?" He grabbed my arm just as I was reaching for my cup. "Right?" His eyes locked on mine. They were tight, hard black knots. "Right?"

I brushed his grip off, lifted the coffee to my lips and stared back at him. "No. That's a fairy tale."

His fist slammed onto the table. The glass in front of him jumped, shivered, and toppled over. "Dammit, it ain't a fairy tale. I don't tell fairy tales."

Hazel rushed to him with a towel. "Easy. Take it easy. Don't bust up this place, please."

"Sorry, I lost it for a minute." His head moved from side to side, as if he were shaking off an image. "Fairy tales. I don't tell fairy tales. Gimme another beer."

I got up. "Harry, you're nuts. You belong in the asylum."

"Wait a minute, Mel," he said, grabbing my arm. "I want to show you something. He reached into a sagging hip pocket and pulled out a pistol. A big one. Black. I jerked away from him.

"What do you think of this?" He waved the pistol. "This'll fix all the capitalists. Right?"

"Keep away from me, Harry. Keep away." I turned and ran up the stairs to my room.

I THOUGHT ABOUT HARRY all night as I delivered beads to the men at the waffle irons. He worried me. Was he simply mad? Was he so captured by the dream of a better society, a socialist America, as to become a fanatic? Or was he an *agent provocateur*? Whatever he was, he could be a danger to me, to George, to Boyd, to everyone else in our little Party group. He could hurt the union, too.

I called George at the union hall after I had a coffee. He met me at the donut shop on West Mechanic Street.

"I don't like it," I said. "He comes on too strong."

George chewed on his doughnut. "I've been hearing lots of stories about Harry lately. About how he gets away with murder on the job. The foremen love him, even when he fucks up. He's fishy, all right."

"He could be a company fink, ratting on the union," I said.

George looked thoughtful. "Could be. But the company wouldn't be interested in revolution. Harry rants about revolution. Could be he's FBI. J. Edgar's always blowing his top about the Reds and revolution. The FBI goes around chasing Reds and all the crooks and con men come out to play."

We agreed that we couldn't be our own FBI watching the big-time FBI. Finally, George said "Let's get him together with me, you, Boyd, Arthur, maybe Nick, who recruited Harry. Let's try to smoke him out. See what happens."

George arranged a party early Saturday night at his apartment. A stag, he called it. He asked his wife, Allie, and Arthur's wife, Ethel, to get all the wives and girlfriends together for their own party.

Each of the men brought some booze. George poured the drinks, and his hand was heavy over Harry's glass.

"Here's to the revolushon," Harry chortled, raising his glass.

"Up yours," George replied, his face suddenly grim, jowls quivering.

Harry gulped from his glass. "What's wrong, George? Whadid I do?"

"You're nothing but a bullshitting revolutionist," George said, his voice between a bark and a bellow. "You're nothing but talk, talk, talk. You know as much about revolutions as I know about flying to the moon. Where do you get off talking about revolutions all the time? Just because you joined the Party doesn't make you a revolutionist. None of us are revolutionists, especially not you." George took a sip of his drink. His hand shook. His face, beading with sweat, was red.

Harry took another long gulp. "Jeezus, George. I didn't say I was a revolushon. All I said was Here's to..."

Boyd stepped in front of George with the bottle. He took Harry's glass, filled it, and handed it back to Harry, who lay sprawled on the couch, a stunned, frenzied look on his face.

"Harry," Boyd said. "Lay off that kinda talk."

Harry nodded, gulped from the glass again, and looked wildly around the room. At Arthur. At Nick. At me. "So what's the big deal? Okay, so I made a mistake about talking about revolushons. Thasall. A mistake. I won't do it again." He hitched himself up on the couch. "Hey, Nick. Tell 'em it's a joke we have. It don't mean nuthin. Jeezus, Nick."

Nick, hunched on a chair across from Harry, hung his head sullenly, not looking at the big man.

"I thought you wuz a buddy, Nick," Harry said, his disappointment dropping to a whisper.

Arthur, the best orator and debater in the union, always strongest on his feet, stood over Harry. Lean and neat, he was known as the New York Dude for his sartorial splendor—even at his job as fabric inspector, where unpressed jeans and droopy shirts were the uniform.

"Harry," he began, his voice high and raspy, "you're always talking about your great granddaddy signing the Declaration of Independence." He cleared his throat. The raspiness eased, the hint of a New York accent emerging. "I thought you were pullin' our legs. But I checked you out. There was a Josiah Bartlett signed the Declaration."

Harry pulled himself up higher on the couch. "See," he said to me, "I tole you."

"But that doesn't mean *you'd* sign," Arthur said.

"Hell, yes. Sure I would. I'd sign it in a minute," Harry said.

"Yeah, but with what name?"

"Whaddya mean, what name? My name: Harry Bartlett."

"Why not your real name…Benedict Arnold?" Arthur paused, waiting for the full effect to hit Harry.

"Benedict Arnold," he sputtered. "The spy? You think I'm a spy?"

He turned to look at each of us, licking his lips nervously. His face hardened. He lifted himself clumsily off the couch and stood before us, wavering slightly. "To tell you the truth, I don't give a shit what any of you think. And I don't give a shit what *you* think, you fuckin' Jew."

Turning to Nick, he said "Let's get outtahere, buddy. Come on. Let's go."

Nick, his face still next to his chest, silently followed Harry out the door.

There was a long silence in the room. There was now no question about Harry and Nick. The only question was the damage they'd do.

I looked at George and Boyd. What would happen to them in the union? And Arthur—would he lose his job? Would I be fired from mine? Communists and unionists, fingered by spies for the bosses and for the FBI, were kicked out of office and fired. It had been that way all through the history of the Party in the United States, and through the history of unions.

Finally, I sputtered: "Jeezus. How did this guy ever get in the Party? Who in hell vouched for him?"

Arthur shook his head. "We didn't know him at all."

George took a sip of his bourbon. "He's a spinner. Always hanging around the hot union guys."

"Yeah, always the first one to bug a foreman," Boyd said.

"That was to show us he wasn't afraid of the bosses," George said. "What a laugh. The bosses always knew what he was up to."

Arthur scratched his head. "He always said he wanted to help make a better world for working people. I guess you can say he talked himself into the Party. And we took him in because we believed his rhetoric."

"Who in hell can you trust?" I asked. "Who in hell can you believe?"

A couple of nights later, the shift foreman and a thin nervous-looking guy came up to me as I unloaded beads from the truck. The foreman jerked a thumb at me. "The office wants to see you." To the thin man beside him he began explaining the duties of a bead boy.

11

ROUNDHOUSE

Somehow I learned about a job at the Western Maryland Railroad and went to their personnel office one morning in the fall of 1947. I was hired for the third shift, from eleven at night to seven in the morning, the graveyard, relieved finally to get a job after two months of unemployment.

I was beginning to believe I'd been relegated to a blacklist of people barred from working anywhere in industry or the labor movement. Just six months earlier I'd been fired from the CIO. "You're a stinking Red," the organizing director barked at me. Four months later, I was laid off at Kelly-Springfield Tire Company. A reduction in work force, I was told. But the company hired dozens of men that same day.

When I filled out the application form in the dingy railroad office on the southern fringe of Cumberland, Maryland, I looked for that $64,000 question: *Are you now or have you been a member of the Communist Party?* That question was to appear on later forms, but it wasn't there this time. The personnel director, sitting in a corner at a relatively clean desk amid an office crowded with grimy file cabinets, glanced over the form and looked me up and down. "If you pass the doctor's exam, you're hired," he said, and waved me to a bench beside a door bearing the sign *Doctor.*

I didn't wait long. The doctor, pudgy, dough-faced, stifled a yawn as he poked my ribs with his stethoscope, had me pull down my pants, cupped my testicles in his hand, ordered me to cough, then probed the groin with his finger, searching for a hernia. That was it. He could have been a meat inspector in a stockyard. I was ordered to report for work in the roundhouse that night.

Cumberland had good bus service, organized to haul people to their three shifts in the Baltimore & Ohio Railroad yards at the northern end of the city, to shifts at the sprawling Celanese mills ten miles in the other direction, to Kelly-Springfield on Mechanic Street, to the Western Maryland roundhouse a few blocks further on.

My new wife Diana and I lived in a one-bedroom apartment in a converted Victorian house on a hill above the B & O station. That first night the bus ride to the roundhouse was quick and direct; there was little traffic and no train blocking the crossings.

So I was early as I walked alongside converging tracks toward the three-story roundhouse. Lights gleamed through the dirty clerestory windows of the circular building. They glinted down on a cumbersome steel turntable in the pit, as if onto a stage.

On a track in the roundhouse, its high ceiling smudged with the carbon of years of engine-smoke and cinders, stood a grimy black locomotive and tender—each cold, lifeless. There was no hissing of steam, no rumble of machinery, no hammering, no voices: only an eerie silence.

I stood uncertainly beside the engine, wondering whether I had the right place. Then I heard a voice. "Hey, you there. Come on up here."

I looked up. A grizzled brown face poked through the window on the engineer's side of the cab.

"Climb up there." He pointed to rungs leading up to the platform of the coal tender in back of the locomotive and quickly slid the window shut.

I swung up the rungs and parted a heavy oily curtain that hung between tender and engine. A small man stepped down from his engineer's seat and held his hand out. "I'm Robert. Robert Parks. You and me'll be working together."

He was short and looked thin and wiry, even in his bulky blue overalls. His striped railroader's cap was pulled down close to his ears, almost down to his eyebrows, accentuating his large, broad nose and heavy lips. In the murky light of the cab his skin had the color and sheen of an old madrone tree trunk—a dusky, polished copper.

I shook his hand, told him my name, and asked what my job was to be.

He stared at me for a moment, then turned back to his seat, nodding to the fireman's seat across from him. "Put your bucket there and sit down."

The light glinted into the cab through the window. I could see streaks of heavy grey sideburns jutting from under his denim cap and a stubble of grey, peppery beard. I guessed him to be between fifty and sixty.

"You're gonna be a firebrick setter," he said, pulling a cigarette from a frayed overall pocket. "I'll show you what to do. Maybe you can do it; maybe you can't. We'll see."

He lit his cigarette. I watched the flickering match flare up and shine on the rows of gauges on the black steel of the engine. The bell and whistle cords hung like tassels overhead. "We got a little time. Shift don't start 'til eleven. Time for a smoke."

I reached into my mackinaw pocket and pulled out a cigarette. As I lit it, Parks stared at me again.

"I got nothing against you," he said, his voice low and raspy. "You didn't pick this job. But I was hoping they'd send me a brother." His head slumped to his chest, and he fingered the cigarette nervously before bringing it to his lips. A chill ran through me. Was he going to turn me down? I didn't know what to say. I puffed on my cigarette and watched him.

He took a long drag on his cigarette and then parted the heavy curtain and flicked the butt into the mound of coal in the tender. He kept the curtain open for me.

"Okay," he said. "Let's see if you cut it."

He reached behind him and picked up a long flashlight and a hammer with a wedge-shaped head. He stooped, lifted the handle on the engine firebox and pulled the firebox door open.

"We're going in there." He flashed his light on the opening. "That's the firebox. We're checking on the condition of the firebrick. I'll show you what's bad, and then we'll get new bricks and put 'em in." He handed me a second flashlight. "Follow me."

He ducked into the opening, laying his flashlight and mallet inside the firebox and pulling himself through the hole. I squatted down, throwing a beam of light on the opening. I knew I'd have problems squeezing through the narrow slot—no more than sixteen inches wide. I took off my bulky mackinaw, dropped it on the seat next to my lunch bucket, and slid through the gap.

Now I was on my knees in the belly of the engine. I was too tall to stand, but Parks could; there at the front of the engine, he held his light up, poking into the curved bricks that lined the long firebox.

"See this?" he prodded a section of brick, watching it crumble, "It's shot." He chipped away at the brick with his hammer. "When it goes bad it gets a certain color. After a while you can spot the bad ones."

He was all business, but I wasn't. I was trying to deal with the intense claustrophobia gripping me. I couldn't tell what he meant by differences in color; they all looked the same to me. All I could see was the long round coffin in which I was entombed.

"But if you can't tell by the color, you can tell by hitting 'em. If they give and you can poke a hole in 'em, it's bad. Like this."

From my knees I looked up at him, trying to keep the slivers of broken firebrick from my eyes, cutting off the stabs of terror inside me. I wanted to get the hell out of there, but held myself back, checking my dread. I told myself that if Robert Parks had been crawling into this coffin for years, I could, too.

"What you do when you find a bad brick is take the measure." From a hip pocket he pulled out a tape, like those that dressmakers use, a hand-sized notebook, and a stubby pencil. "And write it down. You want to get all the bricks right—tight as a whisker."

I nodded and gripped my flashlight. There was nothing else to hold on to.

Parks swiveled his light down to his feet. "You gotta check the grates, too. Sometimes the steel goes bad from all the heat. Not too often, but it happens." He tapped his hammer against the center of one grate. It rang sharply and patches of oxide flicked off. "These are okay."

I crawled along the grate as Parks checked the brick, row by row back to the firebox opening, stopping occasionally to measure for replacements. Then he thrust his flashlight and mallet through the opening and wriggled out. I followed a moment later and took a deep breath. The inside of the cab, its curtain parted slightly to permit cold night air to swirl in, seemed a doorway back to the world.

"Let's have another smoke before we get the bricks we need," Parks said as he sat in his catbird seat. We both lit up. He took a deep puff, blew a stream of smoke toward the curtain, and in his deep, hoarse voice, announced: "It's easy to see why they sent you here. You gotta be skinny to get through that hole. You coulda been the only skinny one they could find."

Satisfied with his analysis, he tossed his cigarette into the coal pile in the tender, shouldered his way through the curtain, and dropped down the rungs to the roundhouse floor. I followed him and saw the rows of shiny tracks radiating around the circular building like spokes on a wheel: the hub was the turntable, a steel bridge across the deep circular pit in the center of the roundhouse.

There was what Parks called a "coming-in track" to the turntable. A locomotive and its tender were driven to this track and the hissing, steaming locomotive stopped at the ashpit. The locomotive fire was quenched, amidst great billows of steam, and hot coals and ashes were shaken and washed out of the grates. The engine was pushed onto the turntable, which turned slowly until it was stopped at an empty track, then pushed off the turntable further into the roundhouse.

On its own track, the locomotive was checked by boilermakers, pipe fitters, machinists, grease monkeys, engine wipers, air monkeys and tiggers, who tightened bolts, soldered leaky pipes, greased the wheels and maintained the water pumps. On the inside of the huge steel boiler that made up much of the locomotive were the firebricks shielding the steel shell from the intense heat generating the steam. Replacing faulty firebrick was the last part of the maintenance operation. In a few hours, the engine would be ready for another run.

Parks walked alongside one track to the edge of the building and pulled back a tarpaulin to uncover layers of firebrick. Referring to his notebook, he selected the sizes needed and handed the bricks to me. They were surprisingly light, made of a porous material, and I could easily carry the stack piled between my hands up to my chin. He carried a few and led me back to the locomotive, where he lifted the bricks to the tender deck.

He pulled the cab curtain to shut out the cold. "Time for another smoke." He drew deeply on his cigarette and coughed heavily. "We got an easy night. No sense rushing things." He leaned back, his right hand fingering a lever jutting out of the deck beside his seat.

I propped my back against the window over my seat, glad to have another few minutes before entering the coffin again. I suddenly blurted what was on my mind: "What did you mean when you said you were hoping they'd send you a brother?"

He cleared his throat and puffed nervously on the cigarette. "Like I said, I got nothin' against you. It's just all those years of the war, four years, I've been working with nothin' but coloreds. All that time I kept saying to myself that maybe us coloreds will get a chance at the good jobs, like this." He shook his head sadly and pulled off his cap, revealing a close-cropped mass of white hair. He suddenly looked very old and tired—much more than sixty.

"Now the war's over. They don't need us no more. Instead of a brother helping me, I get you." He stepped down from his seat and stamped heavily on a floor clamp that suddenly sprang open the firebox door. He parted the curtain to the coal tender and flicked his cigarette away, his signal to return to work.

"You go first," he said, his foot on the clamp holding open the firebox door open. "The fireman uses this when he's shoveling coal in," he explained.

Gripping my flashlight, I squirmed my way through the hole. Parks handed me a couple of buckets, some chisels and mallets, carefully lifted bricks into my waiting hands, and followed me into the long, dark cylinder.

"Watch me put in a couple of these and then I'll watch you," his voice echoed in the chamber. With his mallet, he cracked the broken firebrick into small chunks that he dropped into a bucket. He lifted a new brick up into the gaping space and tapped it slowly and carefully until it settled into place. "See? Fits better than a glove."

On my knees I watched him, admiring his expertise and skill. It took my mind off the sense of doom I'd felt an hour earlier.

When it came my turn to install a new brick, I found it easier to stand and hunch over with my back brushing the rounded sides of the firebrick wall. The new brick slid into position easily. I had a good feeling about getting it right the first time around. I hoped it wasn't beginner's luck.

To my surprise, Parks was quick with praise. "Hey. You're a natural. You got good hands."

I looked at him gratefully; it wasn't often I got praise on a job—especially from someone who didn't want me there in the first place.

He let me finish putting in the rest of the new brick, patting me on the back as I stood upright in the cab and stretched and straightened my shoulders. He showed me where to dump the broken firebrick and returned to his engineer's catbird seat in the cab. "Lunch time," he announced. "And," he added, "we can sit here for the rest of the shift. We're through."

Parks opened his lunch pail and drew out a sandwich and a small medicine bottle, which he uncorked and sipped from. "Ahhhh," he sighed and ran his tongue over his lips, savoring the liquid. He took another sip, corked the bottle and grinned. "My medicine."

He munched on a thick sandwich crammed high with ham and tomatoes. His jaws worked methodically as he stared up at the gauges before him. "I like working this shift," he drawled, his voice deep and rasping. "No one bothers me. I'm my own boss. I can either push myself or not." He bit into his sandwich and ruminated. "This is an easy night. Most nights we have two, three, sometimes four boxes to work on. That's when you hustle."

I chewed on my sandwich and thought I was lucky to break in on a slow night, when I could spend more time in the cab than in the fire-box.

There were a few other nights in the next few weeks when we had only one or two locomotives to check out. On those nights, we sat huddled in the sheltered cab. I could tell that Parks was feeling a lot more comfortable with me; he didn't attempt to hide his run to his lunch bucket. One night he even offered me the bottle.

I took it from him, wiped the mouth with my palm, and sipped, tentatively. Argggh. A bittersweet jolt enflamed my mouth. "Moonshine," I gasped.

He nodded, his face in a big grin. "Made it myself." He took the bottle back and tilted it into his mouth. "Make it in my tool shed. All the neighbors know, but I give 'em some and they *don't* know." He laughed, a grating bark, his mouth opening wide. "Get what I mean?" He handed me the bottle once more. I held my hand against his and turned it back.

"Too much for me," I said.

"This," he waved the bottle in my face, "is the only fun I have." He put the bottle to his lips and gulped. "Helps get me through the night." He shook the bottle in front of me again. His voice became harsh and he glared at me. "It ain't easy living here, where everybody white hates you. Where they get rid of you first chance they get. It ain't easy. You think it's easy?"

I stood up. "Robert! I don't hate you."

"Oh, I don't mean you. I mean the whiteys that keep me down, that had me cleaning toilets for twenty years on this railroad. I'd still be cleaning toilets if there wasn't a war. The best jobs always went to the white man; us coloreds cleaned the crappers. Someone's gotta do it, they said, and that's all they gave us." He snorted angrily. "Then there was the war. And the labor shortage. And we got qualified. Can you believe it, all of a sudden we *qualified?* That's how I got this job. Used to be a white man's job. But now that the war is over, I wonder if I'll get *dis*-qualified." He took a cigarette out of his overall pocket and puffed in silence, smoke hanging over him like a cloud.

I brooded over his statements for several days. "Robert, don't you think the Negro worker and the white worker have the same problems?" I asked him one night. "Like, with the bosses and pay and conditions?"

He looked at me thoughtfully, drew on his cigarette and coughed. "They could be the same problems, but they're not the *same* problems. Mainly it's the color. Mainly it's the prejudice. I've been watchin' all my life and I can tell you the colored will always be pushed aside by the white man *for* the white man. It happened to me. Twenty-six years ago, when I was hired here, they also hired a white boy. Not even born here; his daddy brought him from Poland or Russia. He got chances and got to be superintendent. They didn't give me the same chances; I was the porter. I cleaned toilets, pushed brooms. The white man don't have to worry about color and prejudice."

He fumbled in his lunch bucket, drew out his bottle and nipped on the medicine. "Ahhh," he said, smacking his lips, "a little of this and..." He rested his head against the window, folded his hands over his chest, closed his eyes and drifted off.

Some nights he asked me questions about where I grew up. He'd shake his head as I related my stories: "I sure wouldn't like growin' up in a big city. Too crowded." About my family. "Havin' three brothers must be good. I had six sisters. They're nice, but brothers musta been more fun." About my father: "He was lucky to have a trade. Printing is a good trade. I would've liked that."

But my questions usually got him started. "Lived here all my life, when it was just a railroad town, before Celanese and Kelly. Went to school here, all the way to high school. My folks been in these parts for over a hundred years. My daddy mined coal for Franklin Roosevelt's granddaddy near Lonaconing."

"G'wan. Roosevelt's grandfather owned a mine here?"

"Yessiree. He owned lots of mines. My daddy came because someone told him about good jobs. Turned out to be a scabbin' job, scabbin' on miners out on strike. Only kind of job a colored man could get those days. But it sure beat choppin' cotton in Georgia for six cents a pound." He reached over and drew the curtain tightly when a sharp, cold wind whipped through the cab. "My, it's cold tonight." He rummaged in his bucket, found his medicine bottle, and took a long swig.

"Did it bother him that he was a scab?"

"Bother him! Hell, yes, it bothered him. He hated it, hated taking someone's job. Hated taking the food out of the mouths of babies."

"But it was either them or him."

"That's right. That's the way he figured. He had to feed his babies, too." He lit another cigarette, dragged on it and coughed heavily. "Damn cigarettes. They're goin' to kill me. I ought to quit." He drew back the curtain and flung the cigarette into the tender.

I didn't ask any questions the next night, after we finished setting bricks in two fireboxes. Parks began talking as soon as we sat on our perches and puffed our cigarettes. "You got me thinking about my daddy last night." He puffed; a cough racked his body. "He…he tried to join the miners' union, but they wouldn't let colored miners in. Now, wasn't that stupid. They cut their own throats."

"The mineworkers' union isn't that way anymore."

"I know. They learned the hard way. Colored scabs took their jobs." He fumbled in his lunch bucket and stopped, struck by a thought.

"And I'll tell you something more stupid: discrimination down in the mines. Whites would ride down to the diggins in one car, coloreds in another. Once they was diggin' at the face you couldn't tell a white miner from a colored one."

Parks settled back, ready for his nap. "My daddy always said: 'to hell with the unions; they're as bad as the bosses. They both discriminate.'"

I leaned against the side of the cab and pondered his statement. *The bosses and labor bosses both discriminate. They sure do. Not only against black and brown people, but against people with different political ideas.* I got fired from the union for being a stinking Red. I got fired from the tire factory because I was fingered as a Red by a couple of spies.

I looked over at Parks, upright in the engineer's seat, arms folded, his grizzled brown face puckered in sleep. He'd survived discrimination. Or had he? Wasn't he always looking over his shoulder for the next hurt, the next slur, the next pink slip? Is that what I could expect of my own future now that Communists were the new outcasts?

One night, soon after, as I passed through the gate and walked toward the roundhouse, one of the personnel office payroll clerks pulled me away from the time clock.

"I got something to t-t-ell you," he began. "Here's your pay up to last night. There's a p-pink slip in it. You are no longer working here." He thrust a brown envelope into my hands. "We tried to get you at home. But you don't have a phone. I'm s-s-orry," he said.

I stood in a daze for a few moments, holding the envelope. I opened it. There indeed was a pink slip. Not one of the forms printed and given out by the hundreds; this was a specially-typed form.

"As of this date," it said, "your services are no longer required. Our medical examiner has determined that you have a tendency to hernia on both sides."

I shook my head. *Tendency to hernia.* Every man walking this earth has a tendency to hernia. And if I had this tendency, why was I hired in the first place? The doctor poked me in the groin and wasn't concerned about the tendency then. Something fishy going on here.

Feelings of sadness, anger, hurt and helplessness gripped me. I crumpled the pink slip into a ball. "I gotta see Robert," I told the clerk and turned to walk into the roundhouse. But the clerk barred my way.

I wanted to say goodbye to Robert—to tell him I was a brother.

I NEEDED NO MORE first-hand experience in the early stages of the Great Red Hunt to realize that I wouldn't get a job anywhere in Cumberland. So Diana and I moved to Baltimore. I was hired immediately and fortuitously at Bethlehem Steel's Sparrows Point complex—fortuitous because Diana was three months pregnant.

The Red Hunt became wilder and dizzier in Cumberland. Nick was arrested in Pittsburgh. In his defense, he claimed that a burglary he was attempting was his way of outfoxing the Communists who were after him. The cops let him go.

A year later, Nick and Harry were revealed as FBI informers. They testified as government witnesses against the Communist leaders on trial in New York. The next year, they also testified against George and eleven other Maryland Communists and helped convict them of charges that they conspired to teach the overthrow of the government by force and violence.

12

COILING PIT

I'd often seen the Bethlehem Steel Company plant at Sparrows Point from the highway on the way out of Baltimore. From that distance, the mill looked ugly and forbidding, its towering stacks always spewing plumes of heavy red smoke, its lofty windowed sheds glistening with reflected sunlight, soot and oil. But now, to me and to the 23,000 men and women who worked three shifts, it was where we drew a paycheck; it was bread and butter. For that you accepted the ugliness.

On my first day in February, 1948, after I stepped off the streetcar and passed through the gates, I walked alongside tracks leading to the rolling mill. I followed lines of men in khaki combat coats and Eisenhower jackets, watch caps pulled over ears against the cold, to the clock shed, where I found my numbered card, my name in the corner, and punched in: 6:40. I'd gotten up at 5 a.m. to make it to the mill in time.

A beefy man with blond close-clipped hair, his dark suit rumpled, scanned a list until he found my number and name. "Go through that door," he said, pointing to an opening in the wall big enough to drive a truck through, "and follow that walk until you get to the pulpit. Ask for Steve."

"Pulpit? What's a pulpit?"

Crewcut looked at me with disbelief. "Pulpit, man. It's over the track. You can't miss it. Steve's behind the window there."

I shrugged. If I couldn't miss it, I'd better try to find it.

Through the doorway to my right were the furnaces, their red and yellow flickering glow lighting the pits in which they were imbedded. High above was the roof of the giant shed, hundreds of feet over the

155

soaring brick furnaces, whose mouths were ringed with glowing, raging heat. Against that flaring light, dark monumental slabs of machines pounded and rocked. Clinging to the windowed ceiling above me were long, praying-mantis-like cranes, stopping and starting fitfully.

Men in hard hats, their dark faces covered partially by goggles, were in overalls, sweaters and long asbestos gloves. They pulled and pushed bars like thick logs into furnace cauldrons, sending sparks crackling over the pits. The air, heavy with smoke and heat, held the acrid smell of burning oil and the sharp tang of ozone.

Off to my left were crushed cars, twisted metals, scraps of unrecognizable forms that once had been useful and now were in piles four stories high. Straight ahead was a blackened path, scarred with ruts left by forklifts and trucks. The path paralleled a track made not of rails but of shiny rollers set a foot apart and stretching down half the length of the shed—perhaps a quarter mile. Another shed, spindly, entirely of windows on three sides, stood on stilts beside the track. I guessed this was the pulpit.

One of the two men inside sat before a long panel on which lights flashed above rows of buttons. The other, dressed in a shearling-lined denim jacket and wearing a long-billed hunting cap, stood looking down at the track. He was Steve, the foreman.

Steve shifted a wad of tobacco from one cheek to the other and motioned me to follow him. He was tall, and bent forward slightly. His baggy oil-stained pants, bunched at the waist, accentuated his thinness. He shuffled stiffly along the walk until we came to a deep pit.

"This here's the coiling pit," he said in a voice that had the high nasal sound of the South in it. "When the sheet comes rollin' out, it comes down this here track and goes into this here pit." He pointed to the rollers below him. They were stepped down and banked to form a hairpin curve. "Your job is to make sure the sheet gets into the pit." He picked up a long wooden pole, much like a vaulter's pole. "Use this here pole."

I didn't know what he was talking about. I was supposed to get a sheet into the pit. I didn't know what a sheet was, nor how to put it on rollers that went loop-the-loop down and then up and around the pit.

"I never did anything like this before," I mumbled. "I'd appreciate your showing me what to do."

Steve shifted his tobacco wad. "Wait a minute. I'll go up the line and give 'em the word." He walked stiffly back to the pulpit. I watched him stop and say a few words to two men with oil cans lubricating the rows of rollers. I looked overhead, to where the crane operators lowered round magnets—big as slabs of granite—onto the piles of metal, picking up tons of the scrap, lifting it high while the crane skittered along its rails, then dropping the load into a chute in the furnace.

Steve returned and picked up the pole. "Watch me," he said. He climbed up a ladder to a platform over the track, planted both feet firmly on the platform, and held the pole as if he were prepared to harpoon a whale. He chewed his tobacco slowly and fixed his eyes on the other end of the track. I kept my eyes on him. Suddenly he tensed. I could hear a rumble on the track—it got louder and louder, like an oncoming train. There was a flash of red on the track, and I could see Steve poke his pole down at a streak. With a roar, the streak was swallowed up in the pit, trailed by a wave of billowing heat.

Steve spit over the side of the track as he handed the pole to me and clambered down the ladder. "Nothin' to it," he said. "Jes' keep your eye on the sheet all the time. Thas all."

I stood on the platform with the pole, nervously eyeing the other end of the track, the dark hulk of huge rollers through which the slabs of red-hot ingots were compressed into a thin, continuous sheet. Each sheet was 200 yards long, five feet across, wide as the track of rollers, and a quarter-inch thick.

The fiery end of what looked like a ribbon emerged from the mill rollers as if squirted from a water nozzle. It roared along the track, undulating and swelling like a live prehistoric monster. I poked my pole down on the rearing head. It ducked into the coiling pit and clattered around until it was tightly wound. Like a roll of toilet paper, I thought. Then, still red-hot, the spool of steel was pushed by a giant prod out of the pit and onto a moving conveyor belt.

I just had time to get my pole in the air before the next steel sheet came pounding down the track. I touched its tip as it came toward me. Into the pit it went. All it needed was a touch. No brute force. Nothing to it.

I glanced down at the coil being upended and pushed onto the conveyer, then braced myself for the next lunging streak. The rhythm was set by the button-pusher in the pulpit. He controlled the opposing rollers that squeezed the red slab thin, and when it was the required one-quarter inch, he released it to race down the track. I adjusted to his pace.

I responded to the sounds: rumble in the distance, deep growl on the track, roar as the steel ribbon came close. Down flicked the pole. Clackety-clacking like a rushing subway train, the ribbon wound itself up.

Over the track, I stood as if on a chariot and plunged my lance into the bodies of charging dragons. Each red fire-breather acquired its own personality as it slithered on its belly toward me. One was the pained face of the union president's subordinate who had fired me. Another the tanned and wrinkled face of the Marine warrant officer who made life hell on the troop transport. Another took the shape of the red-haired wife who wrote me 900 letters during the thousand days I island-hopped in the Pacific.

Rumble! Growl! Roar! Pow!

As the steel clacked into the coiling pit and the heat fleetingly enveloped me, I became aware of a chilling cold on the platform. Quick glances told me that both ends of the shed were open. The winter wind funneled through the building. I was being seared for a moment and frozen for the next few. I was glad for my heavy sweaters and grateful to Steve for giving me asbestos gloves.

He came by occasionally to watch me, saying nothing, just standing near the track with hands in pockets, methodically chewing his wad of tobacco, turning once in a while to squirt a stream of juice into the darkness behind him. Aware of his scrutiny, I made a greater effort to handle my pole with deftness and authority. When he left, I resumed my fantasies.

Hour after hour, the track before me rumbled and roared. One minute I was covered with a blanket of heat; the next a chill of biting cold. I plunged the pole onto the head of the rearing steel without thinking about it, a sleepwalker on a platform, moving my hands automatically, hypnotically.

Then, suddenly, my thick glove slipped down as I aimed the pole at the rushing red ribbon. I lost my grip and the pole skipped off the dancing steel, clattering off the track. The red steel came right at me. I jumped back frantically, backpedaled, and fell off the platform, sprawling on the path beside the track, my breath knocked out of me.

The ribbon of steel hit the end of the coiling pit with the force of a head-on auto collision. Its head crumbled; its center lunged up high above the track and hung in the air—a thin, graceful, sculptural loop, its end twisted and shriveled on the platform.

Still on the ground, I stared up at that twisted mass slowly greying in the cold. When I tried to sit up, I realized I was shaking. I turned on my side, away from the platform.

Steve, breathing hard, his eyes anxious, knelt beside me.

"You okay?" he asked. I nodded. He pulled my arm until I sat up. "Sit over there." He pointed to an upturned barrel a few yards away. "I've got to clear this mess." I groped my way to the barrel and watched Steve wave to the crane operator above. Using hand signals, he directed the drop of the magnet onto the crumpled steel.

The noise of pounding rollers and screeching overhead cranes in the mill made conversation impossible. Instructions were passed on with hand signals—an upthrust thumb to raise the magnet, a thumb the other way to lower it, a circling hand to continue raising the load. Steve was the eyes of the operator fifty feet above him. When the load on the magnet was secure, Steve pointed toward the scrap pile. The crane lumbered along its tracks with its load of new scrap dangling under the glare of powerful lights shielded by the undercarriage of the crane.

Steve bent beside the track, over a long box. "Here's another pole," he said. "Hold onto it for a little while longer. We're almost finished running this light stuff for Ford."

I shuffled to the small ladder to step up to the platform. Steve stopped me. "Hey, you're doing good. But watch it. Don't go to sleep. No sense killing yourself." He patted me on the arm, turned his head, spat, then waved his hand at the pulpit operator. The distant rumble began.

I jousted again—with new enemies.

THE NEXT MORNING, Steve ushered me into the coiling pit to another job. I followed him down grimy cement steps into the pit through which ran a wide, belt-like track, clanking and humming as it was pulled into a dark tunnel running under the entire building. Off to the side was the massive coiling mechanism into which I'd guided the ribbons of steel. Next to it was the mechanical arm that pushed the coil onto the conveyor belt.

Nearby, there were five men, hulking in their heavy sweaters and gloves, standing beside a rickety wooden desk covered with stacks of paper clamped on clipboards.

To one of the men behind the desk, Steve said: "Here's another one for you."

"This here's Augie," he said to me. "He's the boss. He'll show you what to do."

He looked down at the papers. "We've got another big run coming. Let's not screw up," he said to Augie, tall with a pinched face and narrowed, wary eyes. As Steve left, Augie nodded and muttered under his breath: "You're the only screw up around here, you son of a bitch."

He looked at me and his eyes narrowed even more. He took a deep breath and exhaled a cloud of steam. I could tell what he was thinking: he shouldn't have shot his mouth off in front of a new man—one he didn't know, one who could be a friend of Steve's, one who could squeal. He shook his head slightly, as if to say to himself *Can't worry about it now.*

"Were you on the platform yesterday?" he asked.

I nodded.

"The stuff we're going to run now is a damn-sight thicker. It won't fly around. We just got to make sure we get the right order numbers on them," he explained. "They're on this clipboard. Your job is to write the order numbers on the coils when they get on the belt. This is what you use." Into my hand he thrust a long pointer with a hollowed-out end. "And you use this paint." He reached into a box beside the desk and came up with a handful of white, finger-length sticks, like pieces of chalk.

He looked at the four other men around him. "We all take turns, regular turns. You're fifth in line, after Gus here." He pointed to a stocky older man whose dark brown hair hung over his forehead from a corduroy cap whose ear flaps tightly clamped his head. "Watch us, then follow Gus," he said as the rumble started at the far end of the shed.

The men moved toward the coiling machine. Augie scurried to the belt, turning on three large fans that stood in a row alongside the belt-line.

The red-hot steel clattered into the coiling mechanism. The roar was deafening. I could understand why Gus wore ear flaps; they were protection against more than cold. The roar stopped. With a thump made louder by the sudden silence, the coil—the size of a barrel—was tipped and pushed onto the conveyor. Cogs in the belt pulled the glowing coil along, inching it slowly toward the dark mouth of the tunnel.

As the coil began moving, one of the men jumped toward it. With gloved hand holding a paper clamped to a clipboard, he began printing a long string of numbers with his paint stick on the side of the coil. He crouched before the red coil, waddling beside the moving belt as he dabbed.

At his back, cold air from the line of fans blasted him. Finally, after one last look at the numbers on his board, he leaped backward, staggered up from his crouch, put a hand on his back for support, and shuffled to the desk, where Augie took his sheet and handed him another one. The man pulled off his heavy woolen watch cap, wiped his face with it and pushed it down over his head again.

The rumble on the track had turned into a roar by then, and another member of the team jumped up to the burning coil as it came down on the belt. He was gangly, wearing a torn red football jersey over sweaters, number 33 emblazoned on back of the jersey. He crouched before the coil as if he were playing tackle on a football team, following the red stack on his haunches, then jumping away like a jack-in-the-box.

I watched the third man. A minute or two later I saw Gus jump in, dab the numbers furiously, and jump back.

I had my production sheet clamped to the board I held. I pressed the paint stick securely into the hollow at the end of the pointer so that it wouldn't slip out. I waited for the rumble and the roar. The steel coil spun around in the coiler, but I shut out the noise, intent on doing this job, testing whatever strength and skill I needed.

The coil tipped onto the belt. I leaped up to it—but, instead of crouching beside it, I bent over. My head was a foot or so above the fiery ring. I pulled back, my eyes watering, welling over. I held the board with its numbers in front of me, shielding my face from the intense heat. I copied the numbers and letters, dabbing erratically with the paint stick, some of the paint running down the red-hot steel, some numbers and letters merging as I waddled and swayed to follow the moving coil.

The numbers were endless. I kept looking at the production order and then at the hot steel for what seemed an interminable time. I couldn't jump away until I'd copied all the numbers, which seemed to grow arithmetically. At last, I reached the final one, dabbed it on the steel and tried to leap back as I'd seen the others do. My legs didn't have the spring; I rolled away, bending back and skidding on my rump. Gus gave me a hand up.

I stepped away from the fans, took off one glove and felt my burning face. I stumbled to the desk and handed Augie my sheet. He gave me another, which I clamped to my board. I walked stiffly, stopping behind Gus.

"Hey, you're staying in there too long. You'll fry yourself," Gus shouted, between the rumbles and roars.

"What can I do? I gotta write all the numbers."

"Memorize the numbers before you get there. Then just print 'em. Look at the board as little as possible." He inched forward behind Number Three man. Gus glanced at his board and I saw his lips move as he repeated the numbers to himself.

Around and round we went, in a dizzying routine, endless and mindless. Memorizing a jumble of numbers and letters and printing them on the circle of steel made no sense. Why not slap a label on the steel? Why not use a signpost that could be placed in the hole in the center?

"There's got to be a better way," I said to Gus during a lull.

He shook his head. "When you've got maybe 2500-degree heat, everything burns up," he yelled.

There wasn't much conversation on this job, except during the sudden breaks between order runs, and the half-hour lunch break.

We sat on a couple of wooden benches near the desk, the five of us and Augie. We all held the workman's traditional black lunch bucket with small coffee thermos in the lid.

If the belt had come to a stop with a glowing coil on it, we considered ourselves lucky. We could toast our sandwiches on an iron mesh screen kept in the desk drawer—six sandwiches arrayed on the mesh, placed on the coil for a moment, turned over for another moment, then redistributed. Gourmet dining in the bottom of a drafty pit.

After I'd been Number Five man on the crew for a week or so, I asked Augie, between mouthfuls, where the coils of steel went in the tunnel.

"To the warehouse. The stuff cools off in there. Takes about a month."

"Then what?"

"Goes to customers—Ford, Baldwin Locomotive, B & O, Chrysler, you name it. Some of it gets cold rolled; some pickled." He poured coffee into his mug and drank.

"Then what?"

"What do you mean, then what? They cut it up for cars and engines and tanks and tin cans. What in hell do you think they would do with steel? Eat it?" His eyes blazed and he muttered to himself, "Jeez, what stupid shits they send me."

He stared at me. "Say, what in hell are you, anyway? Where in hell did you work before?"

"I worked on newspapers, but nothing like a steel mill."

"There's a big difference between selling papers and shovin' steel around. You're in a man's world now," he laughed, pleased with his observation. Then he became solemn again. "What I mean is, what are you? I'm a Serb. Gus here, he's Belgian. Gino, he's Italian. What are you?"

"What difference would that make?"

"Whatsamatta, you got something to hide?"

"It's none of your business."

"Bullshit. You've got something to hide."

"I ain't hiding nothing."

"Okay, what in hell are you, then?"

I swallowed and glared at him. "I'm Jewish."

He yowled, a wolf baying at the moon, and slapped his thigh. "I knew it. I could smell it. A fuckin' Jew. You can always tell a Jew, always asking questions, so fuckin' nosy." He slapped his thigh again and again. "I knew it, I knew it."

He turned and looked at the four other members of his crew, some plainly embarrassed, capping their thermos jugs and placing them back in the lunchbox. Gino, closed his with a snap. "So what?" he asked, glaring at Augie.

"I'll tell you what," Augie said, rising from the bench and scowling at his audience. "He's in the wrong place. Or maybe he's starting from the bottom. And this is the bottom—the pits. But the Jews run the world. And they're goin to run this fuckin' company too."

"Hey, Augie. Your head's in your asshole," Gino shouted. "We just finished a war about this. Six million Jews didn't make it. If the Jews ran this world would they have killed themselves off?"

The rumble began filling the shed. Glaring at Gino, Augie closed his lunchbox, kicked it under the desk. "Let's go," he snapped.

As the whistle blew to end the shift and we marched to the clock shed to punch out, Ben, one of the pit crew, tall, square-shouldered, a mass of black hair capping his round face, came beside me.

"Hey, I want you to know that Augie's horseshit."

I looked over at him. I hoped my look said to him: *Don't tell me. Tell Augie.* I nodded.

Ben had a brown face, and his hair stood up in spiky clumps. "But I never heard of a Jew working in a steel mill," he said earnestly.

"They work all over, not just in stores and offices. Jews gotta have jobs just like everyone else," I explained as if to a child.

"Yeah, I guess so."

We shuffled to the open shed. I found my card and followed the line of slowly-moving men, hunched, lunchboxes tucked under arms, toward the clock in the center. Then Ben again came beside me and we walked silently to the streetcar stop. We discovered that we were waiting for the same car, and that we lived a few blocks from each other.

We sat side by side as the car rocked down wide Baltimore streets. I stared out at the grimy brick houses facing the bleak mill. The houses rolled by, row on row, mile on mile of identical two-story brick structures with three or four granite steps. The grime faded on the buildings as the trolley made its way towards the city center, where we lived. There, the red brick and granite sparkled in the waning winter light. Lace curtains in the windows seemed to be a special wrapping inside the houses. Even the leafless, bony trees, shaking in the wind, looked welcoming.

It was good to be out of the mill, away from its noise, its ominous shadows, its heat, its cold.

Ben, silent, suddenly blurted: "That's the trouble with this world. Too much hate. Hate Jews. Hate Negroes. Hate Russians. Hate. Kill. Hate. Kill," his words tumbling out. "Me, I hate the haters," he said with a big grin as he stood, turned up the collar on his U.S. Army jacket. "I'll see you tomorrow." He held on to the sidegrips on the trolley seats and made his way down to the street.

I MOVED OVER to make room for Ben when he came up the trolley aisle the next morning. His black hair was slicked back and gleamed with wetness. He was shaved and scrubbed, not like many of the men who kept stubbles of beard all week and wore the same workclothes until the stink overwhelmed even them.

"I've been thinking," he announced. "Augie is goin' to give you a hard time. No question about it. But we can't let him get away with anymore of his shit."

"What're you going to do?"

"I gotta talk to the other guys first." He sat rigidly in the swaying trolley seat, lunchbox in his lap, staring at the back of the motorman. I watched the grey streets go by and respected his silence.

In the weeks we rode streetcars together I began to notice that Ben was quiet, somewhat morose each morning. When we headed home at night he was a different man, talkative, sometimes joyous, sometimes bitter.

"Oh, yeah. I psych myself up," he explained. "I try to turn my mind off. It's the only way I can get through the shift."

"I know a guy who worked in the post office," I told him. "He said every time he clocked in he twisted his ear to turn his mind off."

"I gotta twist *both* ears." He grinned. "It gets harder and harder each day." He looked out the trolley window at the blur of houses along Dundalk Avenue. "I've been here three years now. I don't know how much longer I can stand it."

"It's a job. Not bad pay. After getting unemployment for a few months, I'm glad to have it."

"Oh, yeah. Better than no job, that's for sure. But what a price to pay."

"What'dya mean, price?"

"We're whores," Ben said, his black eyes intent. "We don't have any rights around here. We sell our bodies to Bethlehem for eight hours. We give up the right to speak our mind. Can't criticize or complain. These are dangerous jobs but…but we can't talk about the job or the bosses in the mill."

"The company owns the mill. They set the rules."

"Hey, don't I know it. Even the union knows it. And they call this a free country. Crap. It's nothing but a dictatorship."

"Have you tried any other jobs?"

"They're all the same." He stared out the window again. The trolley was clanging down Eastern Avenue, close to his stop. "It makes no sense. Why do we have to give up our rights for the right to a job?" He stood up. "*There's* a good question. Think about it." He buttoned his jacket and slouched to the exit.

I did think about it. I thought that I had accepted the dictatorship of the mill just as I had accepted its ugliness. I was only one of many selling my soul for a job. It's what you had to do. But I worried, too.

Was I going to wind up frustrated or lost like Ben the longer I stayed in the mill?

I tried reading a newspaper during next morning's trolley ride. The shifting lights on the newsprint made me bleary and I gave it up. I fell into a meditative state next to Ben and tried not to think about the job.

WHEN WE GOT TO THE MILL one morning weeks later, knots of men were meeting briefly and breaking apart to join the line trudging along the tracks to the mill. Ben looked at me and mumbled, "Something's up."

He stopped in front of one group. "What's happening?" he asked.

"Some guy got it in the pickling vat last night."

"Got what?"

"Got pickled, that's what."

"Holy, jeez."

He turned, licking his lips to remove the sudden dryness. "You know what that means?" he asked me as we rejoined the line.

"No."

"It means this poor guy fell into the vat of acid and his body was eaten up—clothes and all."

"Jeezuz." I shuddered at the vision of a man disappearing in boiling liquid. I got a whiff of the acid once in a while when the wind shifted, but I'd never been inside the pickling mill. There, the coils of cooled thin steel were lowered by crane into a giant vat, where acid ate away the oxides and scale on the metal to make it into tin. I heard it was a bad job, not only because of the fumes, but also because of the danger of splashes.

We inched our way to the time clock and heard growled comments from others in the line.

"The catwalk was slippery as hell."

"It was at the end of the shift. The guy must have been bushed."

"Anyone know him?"

"The fumes must have got him."

"That catwalk's got a film on it. Like ice."

We plodded under the pulpit and into the coiling pit. As we shuffled down the steps, Ben muttered to me, "You'd think they'd shut the mill down for a day, or even a shift, in honor of this man."

I nodded agreement. "I'll bet if the president of Bethlehem died, they'd shut it down."

"Well, let's see what we can do."

He walked to the desk, where the crew stood around Augie. Ben caught Gino's eye and the two walked away. He talked briefly in a tone that did not carry. Gino nodded and they returned to the desk, where Ben stashed his lunchbox.

"Gino's Number One today," he said quietly as he came beside me. "Follow what he does."

A whistle blew. The mill slowly took on life. Thumps and clangs came from the furnaces and the rollers. Then the low rumble began and grew into the clatter and roar in the pit. Augie switched the three fans on. A red-hot coil dropped down onto the tracks.

Gino hunkered next to the coil, dabbing each letter and number deliberately as he waddled beside the moving track. He was far beyond the reach of the fans, almost to the mouth of the tunnel, when he stopped and staggered back. Sweaty and red-faced, he returned to the desk for another order, and by that time there were two other coils on the track. Ben and Gus moved slowly on their haunches beside the coils. Roger, in his football jersey, took the next coil almost to the tunnel, and I plodded after him. We were together, a union.

Augie handed out new orders as we returned to the desk. "Hurry up, guys," he exhorted. "God damn, you'll miss a coil." His face was pinched even tighter than usual. He paced between the track and his desk.

We kept the deliberate pace. One unmarked coil went up the tunnel. Then another. "God damn," Augie sputtered. "You can't pull this shit. These coils gotta be marked. You're fuckin' me. You're fuckin' the company. There'll be hell to pay. It's my ass." As he raged, another coil went by. Before we stopped for a coffee break, more than a dozen had gone through untouched. It probably screwed up the company's book-keeping, but they didn't lose any steel. They just wouldn't find a few orders.

Augie avoided us on the coffee break. He dug up an old pair of asbestos gloves, grabbed a clipboard, and dabbed at the last coil with his paint stick. He was really in a corner: he couldn't tell Steve to slow down production to keep up with our pace, nor could he let all the unmarked coils go through, though they wouldn't be noticed for a month.

When the steel began running and coils dropped into the pit again, Augie jumped next to the track and frantically painted the order-num-bers on a coil that had been missed. By the time he finished, we were standing beside his desk waiting for him to hand us more order-slips. Three other coils went by unmarked, in the meantime.

Augie realized it was a losing battle. He took off his gloves, tossed them in a desk drawer, opened his lunchbox, drew a cup of coffee, and sipped.

"Okay, you guys. You got me."

"Yeah, where the hair is short," Gus grinned.

"Okay, okay. Whatd'ya want me to do?"

"You lay off us," Ben shouted while another coil was prodded onto the conveyor. "We'll lay off you."

Augie took a sip on his coffee. He looked at us sullenly, jaw muscles straining as he worked to control his anger.

"Okay," he rasped. "Okay. It's a deal. I'll keep my mouth shut."

Ben clapped Gino on the shoulder, almost a hug. He turned to me. "For the guy who got pickled," he said. I wanted to hug both of them.

On the streetcar ride home that night, Ben was alternately elated and depressed. "We got that dammed Augie…and the company. Oh, man…Beautiful." His face darkened, clouded over with a sudden thought. "But it won't do that poor bastard in the pickling vat any good. We didn't even give him a proper burial." He sat silently for a moment. Then, as we neared his stop, he said: "Come on, get off with me. Let's get a drink."

We scrambled off the trolley at Pratt Street, close to the docks and the old Barbary Coast bars and saloons. In our sweaty work clothes and with our black buckets under our arms, this was our kind of place. Through the dark grey of dusk glittered blinking neon signs: *Porthole…Engine Room…Crow's-Nest…* We chose one called *The Meeting Hall.* It was like no meeting hall I'd ever been in.

I stopped short as I pushed open one of the swinging doors and blinked to adjust to the dimness. On my right was a long, ornate bar with mirrors and rows of liquor bottles reflecting muted lights on the opposite wall. Seated on tall, round-backed wooden chairs were men who appeared to be in a state of suspension, their hands wrapped around a beer bottle. They were silent, glancing at us out of the corner of an eye or fixing on our image in the mirror. We must have passed inspection, for the low mumble of conversation resumed as we filed our way past to an empty booth at the end of the room.

"This is the first time we've had a beer together after work," I said to Ben.

"Yep. I know." He swung the bottle to his lips and drank deeply. "Ahhh, that first one is always the best." His fingernail began prying up a corner of the beer label. "You're the first guy I've wanted to have a beer with," he mumbled self-consciously. "'Cept maybe Gino…but he lives in Dundalk." He scratched away at the label. "I got nothin against the other guys…but, hell, just because you work with them doesn't mean you have to live with 'em." He peeled the label off and smoothed it meticulously on the geometric patterns of oilcloth tacked to the table. "You're different," he said, looking up. "You're more than a working stiff." He lifted his bottle again. "What did you do on your newspaper?" he asked, sipping.

"I was a reporter…and feature writer."

"You wrote stories? You can write?" He fixed his eyes on me in disbelief. "Then whatinhell are you doing in a lousy steel mill?" He shook his head. "Jeezus, what I wouldn't give to have a talent like yours…I'd get out of this mill so fast they'd only see a streak of red on the road."

"I worked on labor papers."

"No shit. Hey, that's great."

"The last one…they thought I was a Red, too radical."

I pulled on my beer and gazed at Ben. Somehow, I knew he could be trusted.

"I couldn't be a Red," he said with a frown. "I'm a loner. I can't work with anyone."

"I don't believe you," I said. "Look how you worked with Gino and the other guys today."

"Yeah, but that was something off the cuff." He beckoned to the aproned bartender for another round. "Let me tell you something I've never told anyone else." He lowered his voice and hunched toward me over the geometric oilcloth. "My old man used to be in the Party."

"G'wan," I said. "When?"

"In the Depression. Everyone was Red then."

"Some of it rubbed off on you."

"Yeah." He sipped his beer thoughtfully. "He got his head beat in a couple of times. I'm not ready for that. Besides, someone makes a decision I don't agree with, and I have to accept it. That's bullshit. I get it all day long in the mill. I don't need that when I'm out of there."

"You mean 'democratic centralism'. The minority accepts the will of the majority."

"Yeah, yeah, democratic horseshit. That just means the majority never listens to the minority." He twirled the empty bottle on the table. "Let's have one more for the road."

"What road are you talking about?" I asked wryly.

He studied me for a moment, grinning broadly, his sweaty face shiny in the dim light of the saloon. "Life, man. The road of life." He raised a thumb in the air. "We're all hobos here, anyway."

A FEW WEEKS LATER, on a Saturday when I tried to sleep late, Diana shook my shoulder. "There's someone at the door." I stumbled out of bed, stepped into sweat pants and shirt and groped out of the bedroom, into the living room bright with sunlight, through the dark kitchen to the door to our apartment, the back half of an old Baltimore mansion. Three other floors above us, formerly bedrooms and sitting rooms, had been converted to other apartments. We'd acquired the old dining room, now split down the middle into bedroom and living room, and the pantry, now our kitchen and dining area.

It was Phil, the few wisps of greying hair slicked back on his forehead. "Sorry to bust in like this," he began excitedly. "But I didn't want to phone you…and besides, it's good news." I held the door open for him and followed him into the living room. He swayed from side to side, like a sailor on a shifting deck.

Diana, wrapping a robe around her protruding belly, came sleepily into the room and looked at him warily. She didn't like him and avoided him, she told me later, because of his reputation as a woman chaser. Like the president of the union she'd worked for—and defied—who believed that any woman was fair game.

Phil nodded to Diana, watching her walk heavy-footed and unsteadily to a chair. He turned to me. "The Party wants you to take the job as Washington correspondent on the *Daily*." He smiled, exposing the gap between his two front teeth. "You'll be Rob Hall's assistant."

Dazed, I sat on the cot that served as our couch. My head whirled. God, I'm getting out of that mill…I'm getting out…Going back to newspapers…the *Daily Worker*…the best labor paper in the country.

Frankfeld stood over me, grinning. I grinned back, suddenly feeling that a ponderous iron door in front of me had been pulled open.

13

CORRESPONDENT

I commuted on the B & O morning express to Washington five days a week for more than a year, invariably sitting a few seats away from Senator Millard Tydings, the Democrat from Maryland. He didn't know who I was, but we had the same routine.

Each of us would read *The New York Times* during the hour it took the train to reach Union Station, then trudge up the hill to the Capitol, he to his Senate office, I to the House Press Gallery. He was a vigorous walker, but I was younger, faster, and motivated to prove that I was as good as any senator—at least in hill-climbing.

I'd look over the list of scheduled hearings and press conferences and call my boss, Rob, to choose stories to follow that day.

Rob, in the *Worker* office of the National Press Building, would have checked the Associated Press ticker in the Press Club's restaurant while he was having his coffee. In his deep Southern drawl he'd suggest, never order, an area of concentration. He was a news hound, a reporter for more than twenty years, and could smell a story. His instinct and knowledge of Washington politics set our story agenda for the day.

We'd try to find stories of importance and meaning for our radical readers involved in the labor movement or in social and political activities. Often we dug up stories and angles that other newspapers buried or ignored.

This was the Truman Era. President Harry Truman felt he had to prove himself, and launched a simultaneous Cold War against the

Soviet Union and the labor and left-wing movement in the United States.

There were more stories than we could handle: Truman's executive order requiring a loyalty oath from all government employees; his creation of the National Security Agency and CIA; hearings by the House Un-American Activities Committee; the Congressional battle on renewing the draft; the passage of the union-breaking Taft-Hartley law and its subsequent veto—then acceptance—by Truman; the struggle in Congress over the Mundt-Nixon bill, which outlawed the Communist Party; the Hiss-Chambers hearings conducted by Congressman Nixon, who, Cinderella-like, turned Pumpkin Papers into a chariot to the White House; on and on, amid scandals of bribe-taking by a host of Truman henchmen.

Whatever story it was, we met each afternoon at the *Worker's* Press Building cubicle in downtown Washington to pound out our copy on our ancient typewriters. Rob's clattering had machine-gun rapidity; mine was limited by my two-finger agility. We'd toss our copy to each other for editing, and then one of us would retype the stories on the teletype linked directly to the *Worker* office in New York. We'd generally finish by deadline—four o'clock—then retire to the Press Club for a beer and post-mortem. If the mortem required more discussion, we'd hoist a few more beers.

I followed this routine with Rob for four years. Ten years older, he became my mentor and best friend. Tall, greying and shaggy-haired, he was never without his pipe hanging out of the right side of his mouth.

Born in Mississippi, he'd been a full-time reporter in Mobile, Alabama before quitting to study at Columbia University. There, in 1932, he became a leader in the student movement and a member of the Communist Party. After graduation he returned to the South to help organize sharecroppers and oppose segregation and the poll tax, writing vividly in the *Worker* of these struggles in the South. When he was discharged from the U.S. Army in 1946, he was named the *Worker's* chief Washington correspondent.

Amiable, quick-witted and analytical, he had constant battles with the hide-bound and fearful board of editors in New York and their bosses, the Communist Party National Committee. He was in constant hot water. The beer he imbibed sometimes helped cool that water, but the graphic stories and columns he wrote only heated it again. It was ironic that while life around us in Washington swirled from top to bottom with anti-Communism, the Party leadership indulged in unhappy, bitter backbiting.

At the same time, Rob's personal life soured. He became estranged from his wife, Clara, then enamored with Mickie, a dark-haired young woman who worked as a teletypist in an office across the hall from us. Mickie became almost a fixture in our tiny office.

Life was hectic for me as well. Diana gave birth to our son, Michael, on August 10, 1948. When Michael was six months old, we moved from our flat in the Baltimore mansion to a small apartment in a building next to Rob's in a Southeast Washington housing complex. Many of the residents were unionists and political activists, and many were the families of enlisted men stationed at a nearby Air Force base. A strange mix: oil and water.

Usually bright and cheerful, Diana became taciturn and morose as she acted the housewife and mother and worried about friends who were losing their jobs under the anti-Communist assaults from the White House down. "What do we do with the baby if you and I get arrested?" she'd ask in a kind of weary litany. I had no answers. Best I could come up with was, "My mother will take care of him." She'd shudder.

Diana had left her Berkeley home at eighteen to escape a constant and escalating battle with her stepmother. She didn't want her son raised by another surrogate mother.

Rob and I were all over the place, covering the Senate and House and their committees, the Supreme Court, the Justice Department, the Labor Department and the White House. Rob usually went to the State Department. At Truman's press conferences, at that time held around his desk in the Oval office, Rob and I were usually flanked by two or three burly men who never took notes.

The biggest story I ever covered involved seven black men in Martinsville, Virginia who were charged with raping a white woman. Each was found guilty in one-day trials and sentenced to death. I saw a report of their trials in the *Afro-American*, a weekly newspaper, and drove to Southern Virginia in a borrowed car. For two weeks I roamed the small industrial city, its black community frightened almost into silence—especially its church leaders. In a series of articles I exposed the racist façade behind the trials, the lynch atmosphere in the city, and the appeals of innocence by the seven men.

My stories galvanized *Worker* readers into taking up the cause of the Martinsville Seven. Defense committees were organized, rallies were held, and booklets about the case were distributed by the millions. In a few months, committees in Europe, Japan and several African countries became involved in the struggle to save the men. But after numerous court appeals during a two-year battle, all the men were electrocuted in the Richmond penitentiary.

I was so devastated by the outcome that I could not cover the electrocutions; Rob went instead.

IN THE MEANTIME, Senator Joe McCarthy took over the Communist hunting campaign from President Truman and turned Washington into a demoralizing, spooky city. It was discouraging to cover McCarthy's press conferences, crowded with experienced, intelligent reporters, and watch them swallow his lies without question.

And when the Korean War broke out, newsmen who had nodded cheerily each evening as we went up to the Press Club for a drink now turned away. In the House and Senate press galleries it suddenly became difficult to get information. Senators and representatives who had talked to us freely now turned their backs.

But we weren't pariahs to one representative, Vito Marcantonio of New York. He was a pariah himself to most of the members of the

House and Senate for his outspoken frankness. Very few of his colleagues would associate with him. He rarely got invited to Washington power socials. And he hated to sit around his hotel room or hang out in a hotel bar in the evening. When he got particularly lonely, he'd invite Rob and me out to dinner.

We went to a fancy restaurant one night. There, seated at a table to the right of the entrance, was J. Edgar Hoover and his constant companion Clyde Tolson. Marcantonio stopped, nodded graciously and said: "Good evening, Mr. Director." Hoover paused for a second, tightened his bulldog jaw, and bowed his head slowly in response. Marc smiled, turned and walked away. *Sotto voce*, as we walked to our table, he hissed: "Fuckin' fairy."

Rob got a six-week leave of absence to fly to Reno for a divorce. Those six-weeks were a nightmare for me. I tried to carry Rob's beat as well as my own. I was saved from being a total wreck by Mickie, Rob's friend, who frequently sneaked away from her office to teletype my stories to New York.

But I came closest to breakdown when Diana moved away from me. She took Michael, his crib, and a few suitcases, and moved into a downtown basement apartment.

Rob returned from Reno, married Mickie, and moved out of the apartment complex. No longer did we go to work together on the bus. With Diana and the baby gone, going home to an empty, cheerless apartment was oppressive. Those things, big and little, added up.

Then came the blow that laid me low. The anti-Communist barrages by Truman, McCarthy, the FBI, the establishment press, and every politician in between had choked off support and contributions to the *Worker*. The editors cut expenses. Instead of "downsizing," they transferred me to New York. Even though I'd been born there and had lived there for more than half my life, I hated that city, and had always tried to run away from it.

I hated working there. I was a stranger in the dingy city room, my attitude reflected in the banal, uninspired stories I turned in. When I was fired I felt liberated.

14

NEW YORK CENTRAL

I changed my name to Frank Melvin in 1951, hoping to change my luck and my life.

The alteration was easy. I applied to the Social Security Administration for a number under my newly-adopted name, and a card was mailed to me at a New York City address.

But I didn't ask Social Security for luck and spirit; these weren't in the SSA's handbook of available services. I needed both, because I'd lost love, marriage and job in a matter of months.

During our life together in Washington, Diana had become fearful and withdrawn. She worried over the newspaper headlines screaming about Reds fired from government jobs, Reds kicked out of union positions, barred from teaching in schools, about top Communist Party officials arrested and convicted. She was a Red. Where was she to go? What was she to do?

We tried to talk about it. It was difficult, painful. I tried to convince her that you don't—*you can't*—run in the face of the enemy. A foolish, foolhardy position, I now know. She resisted my arguments. Eventually, she couldn't and didn't talk to me. When she took the baby and moved from me and the Anacostia apartment, I was alone with my beliefs.

There was, moreover, a practical side to adopting a new identity. It was a way of dodging the FBI's ritual of tracking me on the Social Security rolls, then visiting my employer and suggesting that I be fired. It had happened many times in the past to other radicals, and a few times to me. Besides, my new name, Frank Melvin, had a nice ring to it and it was true—sometimes painfully.

While awaiting my new Social Security number, I dug ditches for a construction contractor working for the telephone company. I rented a room from an elderly couple in an apartment near Broadway and 100th Street and got up at five each morning to meet the construction company foreman, who drove me to the job in the far reaches of Queens.

I was lucky to get the job. Mike Singer, the *Worker's* City Hall reporter, knew all the politicians and wheelers and dealers—among them the owner of the construction company—and got the job for me. From seven in the morning until three in the afternoon, with a half-hour for lunch, I swung a pickax and hefted a shovel gouging a deep ditch in Corona streets a few hundred yards ahead of another crew connecting heavy rectangular tile to hold strands of telephone cables. After a few weeks, my arm muscles and back stopped protesting and I began to feel healthy and strong.

I made more money digging ditches than I had at the paper. I saved as much as I could, knowing I needed a stake if I was to move on to another way of life.

It's not often that people get a chance to change their lives, I thought. Most people in New York City merely exist from day to day, paycheck to paycheck, hating what they do and unable to quit their jobs. I told myself I didn't want that kind of existence.

I didn't want any more politics, either—though I hadn't figured out how to avoid them. As far as I knew, everything was politics. Even the ditch digger's job. I just didn't want to be a Communist party member anymore; I wanted to get off the playing field and view the struggle from the bleachers.

Membership in the Party entailed a selfless devotion that most people could not understand. A party member spent hours, never-ending time, sleep-consuming time, speaking to people in unions and key community organizations, trying to convince them to take certain positions—part of the huge jigsaw puzzle in which unions and organizations would fit together and become the fulcrum, the moving force, that would change history. But I didn't want to be a mover of jigsaw pieces; I wanted to be part of the jigsaw, a member of the working class.

Digging ditches was a start, but one day in July, after several months in the long trenches, through rain and scorching heat, I quit, packed a small suitcase, returned my apartment key, took a subway downtown to the 42nd Street bus depot, and bought a ticket to Rochester. Just before boarding a bus, I called my father.

"I'm leaving town. I don't know when I'll see you, but I'll write."

"Where you going?"

"I don't know."

"What're you going to do?"

"I don't know."

And I didn't. New identities are untried, unfettered, unfolding.

I chose Rochester because an old college friend, Kate, lived there with her husband. I hadn't seen her since our days as classmates at Ohio University. I didn't know whether she'd welcome me or send me packing.

The night-long trip on the New York Thruway with its border of trees led westward through small towns drowsing under streetlights. The bus made a brief stop at the tired-looking depot in Syracuse, then went north to Rochester.

I called Kate from an outdoor phone near the station. "It's Mel. Can I come by this early?"

Kate was dressed in a worn bathrobe trailing to her slippers when she answered my knock on the front door. Her full face flushed when she saw me.

"Oh, mygawd. I never expected to see you again, after all these years. What is it, ten years? Come in. Come in." She held the door open while I maneuvered my suitcase through. She bustled me into a dark living room, past a dining table piled high with folders and papers, and into the kitchen.

"Mygawd, it's so good to see you." She paused and stared fixedly at me. "Are you in trouble?"

I shook my head. "Oh, good," she sighed. She poured me a coffee and set it on a table in a sunny bay. "How long will you be here? What *are* you doing here, anyway? What have you been doing?" She stopped suddenly, struck by another thought. "Are you going underground?" she asked, almost in a whisper. "Has the Party sent you underground?"

I shook my head again. "I'm not underground, but the Party doesn't know where I am." I sipped my coffee, told my story and asked for help in launching my new life. "First, I need a job. Then I need a place to live. The rest will follow. Any ideas?"

Kate laughed. "I'm with you. Let me find out who's hiring." She went into the dining room, apparently an office as well, and I could hear her dialing the phone and speaking briefly, in clipped, hurried tones. Almost before I could finish my coffee, she was back with a pad of notes.

"Eastman Kodak isn't hiring. There are three electrical plants around here, but they're laying off. The New York Central yards are about the only place you can get a job quickly."

"What do they do at New York Central?"

"Build freight cars."

"Freight cars? I'm not a machinist."

"Don't have to be. All they want are laborers."

I stared into my coffee cup for a minute. "Okay. Can't hurt to try. Where do I go?"

Kate directed me to the East Rochester streetcar line. Once away from the city, the trolley ran alongside country roads where most of the one-story bungalows and two-story frame homes were painted dull red.

The trolley halted at the road leading to a high gate bearing the sign *New York Central Railroad*, white letters on a dull red background.

Near the gate was a string of freight cars, newly-painted, their white letters shining through the red.

Up the road were the company offices, and through the windows I saw rows of drafting tables and men sitting on high stools, bent over sheets of paper spread over tables. In the employment office I was given an application. I pulled my new Social Security card from my wallet to glance quickly at my number. I'd concocted a high school background and work history that Kate, with her knowledge of local schools and companies, contrived with me, and handed the form to a secretary, who told me to wait.

Ten minutes later I heard the name "Frank Melvin" called. "That's me," I thought. In a small office, a stocky, dark-haired man, shirt-sleeved arms resting on his desk, fingered my application and looked me up and down.

"We happen to have a job open right now, if you can pass the physical." He waved an arm toward a chair near his desk. "Sit down."

"What kind of job is it, and how much does it pay?"

"It's with the painting crew. It pays $2.50 an hour."

I did some quick calculations. For a 40-hour week that was $100—twice as much as I'd made on the paper.

"Sounds good."

He directed me to the doctor's office. There, after a cursory exam like the others I'd taken, I was pronounced fit.

The hiring boss swiveled in his chair behind the desk and glanced at the report. "Can you start tomorrow?"

"Sure."

"Be here at this office at seven-thirty. I'll take you to the painting station myself. Bring your lunch."

I kicked up some dust in the road as I went through the gates and waited for the trolley back to Kate's house. *Damn.* Frank Melvin was *magic.* No sweat. Frank Melvin got a job. Immediately. Luck was changing. Life was changing. Fast. Just six hours after hitting Rochester.

I walked into Kate's house with the news. She was elated.

"But now I've got to find an apartment."

"Have a beer. Let me make some calls."

Kate was magic, too.

I remembered her at Ohio University. Short, plump, stubby fingers, piano-stump legs, a moon face; she charmed with a smile, won you over with an irresistible laugh, an easy competence, a good-natured banter. Her personality overcame any physical shortcomings. Dozens of men were attracted to her, me included, but she had her eyes only on Ted, a steelworker's son from Cleveland, a good-looking blond Slav, poor and dedicated to the union movement.

"I think I found just the place for you. Not too far from here. Right on the streetcar line. It's a one-room apartment with a bathroom and kitchen. Furnished."

"How much?"

"Forty a month."

"Hot damn. Lead me to it. "

I gave the landlady the first month's rent as soon as I saw the place—a long room under the sloping eaves of an old Victorian mansion. One of the closets had been converted into a tiny kitchen, with refrigerator, stove and pantry space arranged like a ship's galley. Pots, pans and dishes were on the shelves. Along a wall, opposite a long, wide-curtained window, sat a couch that served as a bed. Chairs, lamps, a table, and a small chest of drawers were arrayed around the couch. All I needed were some sheets and towels.

Luck was sure riding high. It held out a little longer when Kate gave me some old sheets and towels she didn't need.

THE ALARM CLOCK RANG me awake at five. I fumbled into old work clothes I'd brought—jeans, sweatshirt, sweater, sneakers. I clapped together a couple of sandwiches of prosciutto and provolone cheese I'd bought in an Italian deli, stirred hot water into instant coffee, drank a cupful and poured the rest into a thermos jug that came with my new lunch bucket. My breakfast of bread and cheese and coffee was enough to help ease me out of the apartment, quietly down the stairs to the dark broad porch and out to the streetcar line.

I was half-asleep on the ride out Penfield Road. The houses along the road, so sharp yesterday, were a blur, a swash of gray in the dawn. Inside the yard, a mist shrouded the new freight cars on the track. Lights were on in the drafting room, but not in the hiring office. I was early.

I sat on the steps for a while. As the mist evaporated I could see men slowly coming up the road, lunch pails under their arms. I followed a pair to a set of lockers at the end of an open shed. They sat and talked and smoked, waiting for the shift to begin.

The high shed covered a set of tracks on which eight pairs of steel wheels rested. Further down the tracks was the frame for the wheels and the floor of the freight car. My eyes followed the track to where the steel sides were bolted to the floor-frame and to where the steel roof was lowered to the sides. That's when it began to look like a freight car.

Morning light was strong now, and from the activity on the assembly line I knew it was almost time for the shift to start. I hurried back to the employment office. The hiring boss, a Mr. Swett, pronounced *Sweet,* had me fill out other forms, then led me to the job.

We walked alongside freight cars without doors, cars whose raw gray steel sides were covered with grease and welding alloys, other cars with clean, shiny steel ready for paint and insulation. They towered over us.

Swett brought me to a small group of men standing at the end of the line. They were dressed in jackets and sweaters coated with the same dull red paint I'd seen on the houses of East Rochester. It was called New York Central Red, I learned later. Two wore stiff red burnooses around their heads and over their chins. Two wore scarves covering their heads and jackets coated with dark oily streaks.

"Joe, this is Frank," Swett introduced me to the lead man. "Show him what to do."

Joe, wiry and shriveled, shifting a twisted black cheroot to the other side of his mouth, looked at me standing bareheaded and sneakered. "Sure, boss. But he ain't got no hat and no shoes."

"You're right. Find him a hat." He turned to me. "Get some steel-toed boots for tomorrow," he ordered.

I shifted uncomfortably from one foot to the other while I stared unbelievingly at this motley crew I was to be part of. Joe, small, dried and dark as a pecan nut, went off to a shed to rummage for a hat. He himself wore an aviator's helmet with straps under his chin. The others, their heads covered with paint-spattered scarves and hoods, could have been pirates or highwaymen. All wore tattered overalls stiff with paint.

I watched them as they moved woodenly in boots caked with layers of paint and tar. Two men crawled up a ladder, hauling a long rubber hose to the freight car roof. A third man, standing beside a compressor near the tracks, adjusted some knobs. The two men threw oily scarves around their necks and faces, and one triggered a burst of rubbery tar from the hose, covering the rooftop inch by inch. The tar clouded the air black, misting and drifting to the ground.

Joe handed me a dirty watch cap, which I pulled over my head and ears. He stooped beside a large steel drum labeled *Naphtha* on a wooden horse and drew two buckets of the dark liquid. The one I carried sloshed around, smelling faintly like gasoline, as I followed Joe up the track to another freight car. Joe turned back to a shed near the barrel, pulled two mops and two long poles from it, and marched back to the car.

With two fingers, he removed his cheroot from the corner of his mouth, spat, and announced: "We wash car inside first. You watch." He clamped his teeth around the cheroot, screwed a pole into the mophead, dipped the mop into a bucket, and swung it back and forth from the top of one steel panel to the bottom, as if he were washing a window. Grease and tar, dislodged by the mop and naphtha, slipped down the panel.

"Hey, Frank, you take this side," he motioned to the panels at his back. I soaked the mop in the bucket and screwed the handle into the head. The mop was heavy. It took all my strength to swing it to the top of the panel and keep it from falling to the ground while I tried to shift it back and forth. The naphtha dripped down on me, into my eyes. I had to stop, hold the pole aloft like a flag carrier and shut my eyes for a moment.

Joe did one whole side of nine panels, including the spaces above the doors, while I struggled to complete three. I couldn't control the mop; it wavered and went off at angles as if it had a mind of its own.

Joe chewed on his black stringy cigar, spitting out bits and pieces, and watched me. "Hold your hand here," he suggested, moving my left hand higher on the pole.

I nodded gratefully to him as the mop came under control. He followed me and tidied up the lower sections of my panels.

"Now we go outside, *paisano*." He jumped to the ground, lowered bucket and mop down and turned left. "You take this side." He nodded to the right.

I watched him as he swung his mop high in the air to reach the top of the panel, a good four feet higher than it was on the inside of the box. He held the mop handle with one hand and waved the mop back and forth like a feather duster. The steel shed its grease and oily film as he shimmied the pole down. A few drops of naphtha sprinkled down onto his shiny black leather helmet. Except for the cigar poking out of his mouth, his head under the helmet looked like that of a turtle.

I tried to control the mop-head as it turned and swiveled and dipped like a kite in the wind, until finally I just let the mop follow its own course. I hung on down to the end of the panel and dropped the mop into the bucket. Again and again I lifted and guided, letting the mop make its own way to the bottom. I may have missed some spots, but you had to look closely to see them.

Joe, of course, was ahead of me as we circled around the car. But we met in the middle panel on the other side, and I followed him back to the shed with my bucket and mop. He peeled off his helmet. Scratching his head, he rumpled the gray hair plastered down over his whitish brow. His sun-browned nose was truly Roman, straight and long, classic. He pulled a ropy cigar from an inner pocket, walked a few paces away from the naphtha barrel and lit up, drawing the first puff heavily into his lungs, exhaling a stream of wispy smoke.

"Okay, Frank. You take it easy in this job, you be okay." He puffed on his rope. "No kill yourself, *capeesh?*"

I nodded and picked a crumpled and wet pack of cigarettes from my pants pocket. I looked at it in disgust. How did it get so wet? Then I felt my sweater. It dripped with naphtha. My jeans, sopped. I pulled off the borrowed watch cap and wrung it out. If I'd lit a cigarette I probably would've torched myself.

Washing down the boxcars with naphtha was the first stage in the painting process, the last step in the assembly line. The steel panels were cleaned enough to accept black rubbery insulation on the roof and inside, and dull red paint on the outside. Joe and I were responsible for this preparation.

Tony and Pete were the insulation sprayers. Lou filled up the tanks and watched over the compressor. John and Tom painted the cars New York Central Red, making sure that they used up only half of the five gallons in each paint bucket so that the other half could be reclaimed, without the company's knowledge, on East Rochester's homes. They finished the cars by spraying half a can of white paint on stencils with the railroad's name, logo and car number; the other half became the white trim on the town's homes.

Joe and I sat on upturned paint buckets and watched the two crews tackle the car we'd just cleaned. Pete sprayed a storm of fine black mist as he nozzled the inside of the car. He emerged dripping. After stripping his scarf from his head and face, his eyes looked as if he'd painted kohl around them.

As we watched John and Tom lug their long lines and nozzles to the waiting car, another car slipped down the track, gliding slowly to a stop a dozen feet away. A roustabout on top of the car spun the brake-pinion tight, clambered down the rungs on the end, and slipped a wedge under a wheel.

"*Numero due,*" Joe said. "One more to go today."

John and Tom, taking different sides of the car, swept their red paint on with long steady strokes, a panel at a time. Another fine mist spread through the air, glistening the ground and patches of grass on a small hummock beside the track.

Joe clamped his helmet on, bit down on the end of his cigar, dragged his bucket to the naphtha barrel for a refill, and walked with it to the second boxcar. I was right behind him, and we mopped back to back on the inside of the car, an easy, swinging rhythm, unhurried and steady. As we climbed down to the ground, Joe leaned the mop against the car, pulled off his helmet and walked to the shed. "Lunch," he announced.

We sat on upturned paint pails to eat sandwiches and swig thermos coffee. The sun was high overhead, quickly drying the dew of black tar and red paint that surrounded us. In the bright sunlight, without burnooses or hoods, Tony and Pete and Lou and John and Tom and Joe looked like ordinary blue collar workers, the kind you see in all mill towns.

Tom, short, young and swarthy, waved a clove of garlic under Joe's nose. "Giuseppe—like they say in the old country, a garlic a day keeps the ladies away."

"Mosquitoes, Tommaso—mosquitoes. Not ladies," Joe barked with a laugh, unleashing a string of curses in Italian. I couldn't understand him, but the other men clapped their knees and howled.

Tom grinned. "You got me there, old man." He popped the clove in his mouth and then bit down on a sandwich. He looked around the circle and held out a handful of cloves. "Help yourself, Frank."

"No, thanks. I only like it chopped up in spaghetti."

"Try it," Tom said, poking a clove into my hand. "It's healthy. Good for your system."

"Watch him, Frank. He's a health nut." Pete, short and dumpy-looking in his baggy overalls, grinned at Tom. "He don't eat meat. Something's wrong with someone who don't eat meat."

"Eat this meat, Pietro," said Tom, cupping his crotch.

I felt accepted in the circle under the sun in that yard cluttered with wheels, steel plates, rods, paint cans, upturned barrels and drums, amid stacks of lumber scattered through the woeful stand of tattered trees and bushes, and beside those high cars big as a house.

Three o'clock came quickly that day. I watched the paint crew strip off their spattered overalls, hang them on nails in the shed and change their shoes. I could do neither. I squished down the road to the street-car stop, my sneakers soaked with naphtha. My sweater and jeans smelled but were almost dry.

Tom stepped beside me. "There's a store down the street. You can get shoes there." He walked with me to the East Rochester Men's Store. They had size twelves, denim overalls, heavy denim jackets, and woolen socks. I wore them all to my new home.

After a shower, while waiting for a can of chili to heat up, I stretched out on the couch and felt wrapped in the cocoon of my apartment, warm in the late afternoon sun. With the window open, I could hear birds chirping, and the sounds of distant cars. For the first time in months I had a place of my own.

Was that progress? Maybe. I'd moved from a room to an apartment—certainly a step up. The room had just been a place to sleep. Was there any difference here? I felt a sudden cold bleakness in the narrow apartment—bathroom at one end, kitchen at the other, an oppressive stillness between. Damn. I missed my wife, crazy as she had been. And Michael, my boy, tottering stiffly on spindly legs, clinging to me, climbing onto my lap.

I can change my name, I thought, change my place, but I can't change my memories and my needs.

"LET'S CELEBRATE," I told Kate on the phone. "I got my first paycheck. Let's have dinner and a few drinks. It's on me. Can you and Ted meet me at the Highland Park Inn?"

"With bells on. It'll be good to eat out for a change. We haven't been out in months. I have to find a babysitter, but we'll be there."

I sat at a table just opposite the dark mahogany bar and had a pitcher of beer waiting for them. They walked in hand in hand. Ted, blond hair awry as he took off his hunter's cap, looking chunkier than he had twelve years earlier in college, pounded me on the back.

"Good to see you. Good to see you." He sat heavily in a chair and reached for the beer. "I'm glad things are working out for you here." While Kate took off her coat and adjusted her tightly-bobbed hair, Ted poured two glasses and pushed one to her as she sat down.

"Here's to you," clinking my glass. "Mud in your eye," clinking Kate's glass. He downed the beer in two gulps. He unbuttoned his jacket, draped it over a chair and hunched over the table.

"How does it feel to be a real member of the working class?" he asked with a grin as he filled his glass.

"It's not easy," I admitted. "Especially with winter coming."

"Enjoy it now. "

"Maybe I made a mistake. Maybe I should have gone to Florida or California."

Kate laughed. "You can't win, wherever you go. Don't you guys know that?"

Ted filled our glasses again and waved the empty pitcher over his head to attract the bartender's attention. "Let's drink to the working class, hot or cold." We clinked glasses again.

Ted gulped his beer quickly. "What a day I had today." His fingers played with the glass, spinning out a series of wet circles on the table.

Kate turned to me. "Ted's the only paid organizer the union has. He gets everyone's troubles. Who was it today?" she asked, looking at him affectionately.

"Mary Palumbo. She got a call from her sitter saying her baby was running a high fever and the foreman wouldn't let her go home. So she walked out and the foreman fired her. I spent hours on the phone with all the bosses and finally got 'em to take her back." He gulped his beer and shook his head. "What a bunch of inhuman, unfeeling bastards. I get so dammed tired of fighting them all the time. I'm about worn out."

"Hey, that's good work," I said. "How did you get them to change their minds?"

"I asked them what they would do if any baby of theirs got sick. That made them think. Brought them down to Mary's world."

I emptied the rest of the beer into our glasses and toasted: "Here's to bigger and stronger unions."

Kate raised her glass. "Here's to a child care clause in the next union contract."

The waitress came with another pitcher of beer. "You ready for some food?" she asked, pencil poised over a pad.

"I'll have sirloin rare, with baked potato," I said quickly. "Only the best tonight."

Ted glanced at Kate. "I haven't had steak in a long time. Make mine the same."

"Oh, hell—me, too," Kate echoed.

"If he's trying to spend it all in one night, we'll help him," Ted said to her. "And bring more beer," he yelled at the retreating back of the waitress as he gulped another glass.

"I just think steak is the best there is," I explained. "I always have steak on special occasions. I still remember that steak I had in Washington when I got my discharge from the Marines. The best I ever had. Maybe tonight's will be as good."

"That's funny," Ted said. "I always think of steak not as a reward but as something you give a condemned man on his last meal." He shook his head and stared down at the table and the wet circles. The beer glass spun slowly in his fingers. "I remember the steak they gave us on the ship just before we hit Omaha beach." His head dropped. His lips tightened. He muttered, "I could hardly get it down. I didn't know whether it would be my last meal or…"

His head shot up and he glared around the table. "I don't know why in hell I'm eating steak now," he said angrily. "My gut is churning." He turned. "Waitress. Hey, waitress."

He downed his beer as she came to the table. "Change my order please. Give me barbecued chicken instead of steak." He looked at Kate.

"Yeah, me, too," she said.

Ted filled his glass again as we waited silently for the food. He dropped his head, sunk in his thoughts. Kate peered at him apprehensively.

"Ted, there's nothing to worry about," she said. "You came out of it all right. You're okay, baby." She reached over to him to stroke his hand.

His head thrust up sharply and he glared at her. "What the hell do you know?" he said, his voice low and harsh. "You didn't see those guys. Floating around in the water with their guts out."

Her hand touched his. He flung it aside with a sweep of his arm and Kate shrunk back against her chair. "Oh, Ted. For God's sake. Let it go."

"Let it go. You want me to let it go? I can't," he cried. "I can't forget it." He picked up his glass and tilted it back, staring malevolently at Kate over its edge. "And I can't forget what you did, you bitch."

Kate reached up with her hands and covered her face, moving it from side to side. "No, no, not again," she whispered.

"You fucking bitch," he hissed. "You fucked everyone around when I was over there"

"Oh, no, no," Kate whispered into her hands. She lifted her face, tears spilling down her cheeks. "Ted, let it go. Please. Just remember I love you." She wiped her eyes and cheeks. "Goddammit, Ted. Just forget it. It was a mistake…like your mistakes. Let it go now, please…"

Ted looked at her, his face contorted. He tottered to his feet and flung his glass to the floor. Its shattering brought the waitress and bartender.

"Sorry, it slipped," Ted said, hiding his head in his arms on the table.

Kate put her hand on his shoulder. "Let's go home," she said.

I watched them leave as the waitress came to the table with three plates. I poked at my steak, but it had no taste of celebration.

AS I WENT BACK AND FORTH on the trolley to work that fall and winter, I saw the trees turn from green to yellow to brown. Then I felt the winter winds whip from Canada down over the icy waters of Lake Ontario into East Rochester and the New York Central yards. Only the men at the head of the assembly line had a roof over their heads; the rest of us were exposed to Arctic blasts.

I bundled up in two pairs of long woolen underwear, a pair of woolen pants, a heavy sweater, oversized denim overalls, a heavy lined denim jacket, gloves, and a woolen watchcap, but still felt frozen as soon as I stepped out of my house on the way to the streetcar.

With the others in the painting crew, I huddled around a fire Joe had started in an empty fifty-gallon drum. We were a miserable crew, a wretched-looking crew, dressed as we were in whatever we thought could protect us from the cold.

Tony wore a white parka he'd picked up in an Army surplus store. Pete had a heavy sheepskin-lined coat. Lou wore an old Army overcoat, John an old bulky ski jacket. Tom and I had the sheepskin-lined denims, and Joe had heavy horse blankets.

We'd stand around the fire, huddling as close as we could without getting burned until we had to take our turns at work. Joe, his twisted black cigar in his mouth, would drop his blankets to the ground and jerk his head at me. Then he and I would grab our mops and buckets, fill them with naphtha, and slosh the boxcar interior, moving as quickly as we could. My gloves would always get wet, and I found it best to have another set to wear when I wasn't swinging the mop.

I never timed that frenetic activity, but it couldn't have been longer than seven, maybe ten minutes. By that time, however, I felt like a stalagmite, frozen to the ground. I'd almost embrace the hot drum when I staggered away from the car.

After a while, Joe and I had to do the exterior of the car. I could see Joe steeling himself for the job. He jerked his blankets closer around his shoulders and chin, bent to light his cigar, and puffed nervously until his nostrils produced shafts of thick gray smoke to mix with the vapor of his breath. He stood hunched, his hands crossed, like the figure in the painting of the old Indian huddled on his horse against the cold. I was close to the drum, watching him, waiting for his sign.

When it came, we'd start at the coldest side, where the winds billowed and pulled the icy air around us. We'd stretch and dip our poles then hurry around to the leeward side, the car our shield.

Numbed by the cold, I pulled close to the drum-fire and watched the others in the crew. I realized that Joe and I had the easy jobs. Tony and Pete could barely control the black insulating spray. Most of it was blown away. John and Tom had the same problem when they tried to apply the red cover-coat.

Yet we managed to complete three cars a day, keeping up with the welders and fitters and riveters in that bitter cold. Three o'clock, quitting time, was always a long time coming.

On the trolley ride home one day, teeth still chattering, and in the long hot shower where I could feel ice melt away, I wondered about the job and about myself.

What was I trying to prove? That I was a true working man? That I could shed my intellectualism, my white uncallused hands, by subjecting myself to the toughest kind of job, under the toughest conditions? Or simply that I was a man—not afraid to do a man's work?

Why did I have to prove this to myself? Didn't I have enough problems without taking on this crazy, numbing test? Why couldn't I just find a nice, safe haven and read, and maybe write? I'd wanted to be a journalist and writer since I was twelve. Swinging a mop across rail cars was as far from writing as Lake Ontario was from California. Why did I always hunt out the hardest row to hoe? What was in me that sought wild challenges, the riskiest ways?

By the time I thawed out in the shower, my mind was a jumble of contradictions and uncertainty. I stumbled to the couch and lowered myself to sleep.

WEEK AFTER WEEK, I wrapped myself in layers of my warmest clothes and joined the cluster around the hot drum near the paint shed. It was too cold to banter much, as we had when I first began the job. And it was too cold to eat outside, so I made myself a big breakfast and gave up eating lunch. In my lunch pail I carried coffee in two thermos jugs, and I drew on them all day.

During a heavy snowfall one morning, when the wind piled the snow in layers that almost covered the boxcars, work became dangerous. We couldn't brush away the snow fast enough to mop the cars. Joe and I would try, I wielding an ordinary broom to sweep the snow aside, Joe following quickly with his wet mop. Crystals of snow clung to the wet steel—and to us.

It was worse for Tony and Pete and John and Tom. The insulation and paint they sprayed blew away before touching the steel roof and sides. What stuck became mixed with snow and blistered. They had to return to do a passable job, staying out in the swirling wind twice as long. They were haggard when they finally crowded around the drum-fire.

"Jeezus, what the hell are we doing this for?" I said shrilly, my voice rising, my breath thick as fog.

"Money," Tom muttered between his teeth. "Moola," he added, thrusting his gloved hands above the flames.

I nodded. Sure that was one answer, but it didn't satisfy me. I stamped my feet, encased in two pairs of woolen socks and those steel-toed boots, and thought about sadism as practiced by New York Central.

"I'll bet the bosses would've gone home a long time ago if they had to work out here," I growled. "This is inhumane. Any animal would've gone to his cave long ago."

Tom, standing next to me, turned to warm his back. "One word, Frank, one word tells it all: *production*."

My lips felt frozen. I nodded. Yeah, I thought, that's all the executives in the warm administration building wanted: three boxcars a day, rain or shine, cold or heat, blizzard or breeze. If we didn't want to stick it out, they'd find a dozen other men who would.

"Fear, too," I said to Tom. "Afraid you'll lose your job." He stared at me blankly. He'd forgotten how the conversation had started.

I SAW KATE AND TED almost every weekend. Kate arranged invitations to dinner at the homes of friends and I bundled up, tramped through the snow to their home and we'd go together in Ted's old car. They never said anything about our fateful celebration, but I noticed that Ted had reduced his drinking to a couple of beers a night.

One night we were invited to the home of a woman whom Kate described as a "widow."

"She's a knockout," Kate said, adding, "It's time you started dating." Obviously she worried about my state of celibacy.

Clara, dark-skinned, dark-haired, and curvaceous, lacked only a high comb in her hair to look like Carmen. Her small house, furnished in bright Indian prints and Van Gogh reproductions, had a record collection that filled several bookcases. In the small kitchen nook, lit dramatically with candles, the conversation was gentle and good-humored, and the food Clara prepared—a beef stew with potatoes and kasha—tasted good.

The stage had been set; two lonely people were flung together.

She was as much a widow as I was a bachelor. She had a daughter, eight or nine, a tall Alice-in-Wonderland blond, long-haired, blue-eyed, an expression of dreamy astonishment always on her face. "She looks just like her father," Clara said. "Spitting image."

Her handsome, even beautiful husband, it turned out, was in the state insane asylum, a certified visionary who harbored fantasies, apparitions and at times had fits of violence, beating Clara.

"I still see him," she said plaintively. "Every month. I can't help it. He's like a Greek God...and I feel good that I was in love with a Greek God."

I told her: I'm not Greek. I'm not a God.

She shrugged and looked directly into my eyes. I'll take any man, the look implied.

Through the worst of the winter, I slid into her bed to be warmed and stroked and kissed and embraced, to heave and thrust and lunge, to feel her breath in my ear and her sudden gasping intake, her cry of release, and my own sense of relief, but never the relief of love.

A HUGE SNOWSTORM swept over Rochester one weekend. On Monday morning the snow was piled high around my window and the roofs of neighboring houses. I felt like burrowing into my bed, but I didn't want to lose a day's pay; I took the long trolley ride to the yard. The tracks had been cleared by snow plows, so the streetcar bucked only the white winds to the New York Central stop. I could barely see the administration building when I began trudging up the road: the yard and its line of cars were buried under five feet of snow.

A line of men stamped around the steps of the administration building, Joe among them.

"Hey, *paisano,*" he yelled. "You crazy to come today. No work today."

"I thought maybe we'd get some time in. I need the money."

"You crazy. The company ain't crazy. They no pay for no work."

"It ain't my fault the snowstorm came," I said with a fierceness that startled Joe. "Shit, I need the money." If the truth be told, I really didn't want to stay buried in my apartment any longer.

He glared at me. "Wassamatta with you. You crazy. No one pays for not working."

"Yeah, Joe. I know. But I'm ready to work. I wanna punch in. I wanna work. I'll work out here in this fuckin' snow." I stopped. I suddenly realized I was talking to the wrong man. I should be talking to Mr. Swett, pronounced *Sweet.*

I looked around. Swett wasn't on the steps of the administration building, nor peering out of the windows. The storm had kept him from his job.

Goddamn the fates. Goddamn the storm, I said to myself. Goddamn the company. I shook my head, more to clear it than to rattle a disturbing thought. "You're right, Joe," I said. "It's crazy. No workee, no money. But Swett gets paid. We don't."

Joe shrugged. He looked at me as if to say, 'Hey, that's a fact of life. Them's that has, gets. Them's that don't, don't.'

I stared at Joe and saw his pinched face, his bent body, in a new light: it was me a few years from now, mummified by the cold, twisted by the naphtha and heavy mops, the juices of life squeezed out. I turned, hunched my shoulders against the wind, and walked away.

I waited for the trolley to Rochester. My insides seemed to sag. A heavy sadness, like a swollen cloud, filled my mind. I kept thinking: I don't want to be like Joe. I gotta get out of here. There's nothing here except death.

I brushed the trolley window with my gloved hand and looked out for my stop. The wind whipped snow around the streets and trees, almost wiping away landmarks. I thought: Why am I so glum about not working? I should be glad the company shut down. The cold would have killed us for sure.

I walked in the middle of the street through banks of snow to my apartment. Snow covered the windows and the room was almost dark. I opened one window, and with a broom brushed the snow away. I need another clean sweep, I thought. This life isn't for me. It's hard. Joyless. Dead-end.

I crammed my bag full of clothes and filled some shopping bags with shoes and overalls.

I won't have time to say goodbye to the guys. I don't even know where they lived—never been to their homes, never invited. But they were good guys. I didn't work for the company. I really worked for Tom and Pete and Joe and Lou and the others. We looked out for each other.

I packed boxes with sheets and pillow cases and cartons of cereal and food that I knew Kate could use.

I must say goodbye to Kate and Ted. I love that woman, I thought. Ted treats her like she's a dog. He's a shit. I don't know what I'll do if he lays into her again. One of us will get hurt. Maybe I should have married Kate.

I swept the room, washed and dried the dishes, polished the bathroom sink and cleaned the closets.

But I'm married to Diana. Maybe, after all these months, she'll have me back. Maybe I'll get a chance to play with my son again.

I tied rope around the boxes, put on my heavy denim jacket, and carried the boxes to Kate's house. I was relieved when I found no one there, for I didn't have to explain my sudden action nor make maudlin statements to Kate. I scribbled a note and left it with the boxes on her front porch.

I told my landlady I had to leave because of an emergency. She complimented me on how clean the place was but didn't offer to refund my prepaid rent.

Once I reached the bus station, I took the first one out—to Binghampton.

I stretched out on the long seat across the back of the bus and fell asleep as it pitched slowly along the snow-whitened highway. What should have been a two-hour drive took six hours. I slept so soundly the driver had to shake me awake at the end of the line.

Crossroads: Take a bus to New York? Stay with my parents and get a job in Pop's print shop? Find another job?

Or take a bus to Baltimore, where Diana was? Get a job in Sparrows Point.

The first way is back to the hated existence. The other a hope that she missed me and would have me back.

I bought a ticket to Baltimore.

The bus plodded on through Scranton and the Pennsylvania hills into Harrisburg. I slept again and awoke as we rumbled along the streets of Baltimore in the gray light of dawn.

I found a room in the YMCA on Franklin Avenue that morning. It was just a temporary cell, an address I could give when I applied for a job at Bethlehem Steel. Its main advantage: it was close to the streetcar line to Sparrows Point.

I had no trouble getting a job there. As Frank Melvin I said I'd worked for the New York Central and had quit because it was too dammed cold. The personnel clerk who interviewed me was sympathetic. After a test or two and the filling in of a few forms, he told me to report the following Monday, five days away.

I left the employment office that afternoon feeling that I was back on track. I felt that even if Diana didn't welcome me back, I'd be close to my son and could share part of my life with him and erase some of my loneliness.

That evening I treated myself to a dinner in a downtown restaurant. I passed a phone booth on my way out, and, on a nostalgic whim, looked up George's name in my address book and called.

George had been president of the union at the Celanese plant in Cumberland, then president of the Maryland CIO Council. He resigned both jobs to become a Communist Party organizer in Baltimore.

"What are you doing here? Where are you?" he asked guardedly.

"I got myself a job here," I said. "I'm in a phone booth on Charles Street. I just called to find out how you're doing."

"Where you been? All kinds of shit's hit the fan. Haven't you heard?"

"Heard what?" I asked.

"Never mind. I can't talk to you on the phone. Meet me at the monument on Charles in half an hour."

I sat on the steps of the monument, Washington standing on a hundred-foot-tall pedestal spotlighted from nearby buildings, his shadow falling over a corner of the square.

I watched a car drive up and park near the museum, and recognized George as soon as he stepped from the car. He was tall and heavy; his overcoat made him look wider than he was. I didn't recognize the other man, the driver, until he came closer. It was Roy, the Party organizer from Washington.

George threw his arm around my shoulders and hugged me. "I'm sure glad to see you, Mel. But I wish it were under better circumstances...and better times." He looked around him and frowned.

"Roy," he said softly, "those bastards tailed us. Let's walk and get the hell out of here."

We strolled away from the monument, toward the business district, Roy on one side, George on the other.

"You haven't heard that we got arrested four months ago?" he asked.

"Arrested? Hell, no. For what?"

"Smith Act. Conspiracy to *teach* how to overthrow the government by force and violence."

"That's the same thing they charged Party leaders in New York with."

"Right. They made that charge stick. Now they're trying it all over the rest of the country...here, Los Angeles, St. Louis. "

I looked uneasily over my shoulder.

"The point is," George said as he followed my eyes, "one of the charges against us is that we infiltrated factories and steel mills like Sparrows Point to get a foothold...."

Roy interjected, "...and overthrow the government."

I mumbled, somewhat stupidly, "Can anyone believe that shit?"

"A jury in New York did," George said. He looked over his shoulder again, and pulled us into a dark side street. We walked rapidly.

"Why'd you come back?" he asked.

"I missed Diana and my kid. I thought we could get back together."

He stopped suddenly and put his arm around me again. "You can't stay here," he said softly, almost tenderly. "They're all around. They could pick you up and put you on the stand and you'd have to testify against us."

"I'd never testify against you," I snapped. "Never."

"All they have to do is ask you whether you worked at the Point. That's all the testimony they need."

I looked into George's eyes. "I would have to say I did," I said slowly.

"And that would prove their charge."

"You got it," Roy said.

"And you guys get hung."

George nodded. "You see, you can't stay. You gotta get out of Baltimore." He unbuttoned his overcoat and reached into a jacket pocket. "Here, take this. It's bus fare and enough for a few days to get you going someplace else...."

Numbly, I took the money. "Jeezus, George. I hope I didn't make things worse for you here. I didn't know. I've been in my own world. I didn't know what was going on," I mumbled.

He shook my hand. Roy shook my hand. I stared at them as they turned away and went up a side street. I pressed myself against a building and watched two men cross the street after them.

I hurried along dark streets, turning corners quickly, and backtracking, to see if anyone was following me as I headed to my cell at the Y.

Early the next morning, I carried my bags to the street, hailed a cab and drove to the bus station. I bought a ticket to New York City, and as the bus pulled out onto the rain-slicked highway, tore my Social Security card into tiny bits, opened the window and scattered the shreds like snow.

Frank Melvin was no more.

15

ALEC

A lec told me the story as we sat at Nick's Bar in Greenwich Village listening to Pete Fountain and his New Orleans Five while the rest of the Friday night crowd stomped and beat the tables in accompaniment. He had to yell to make himself heard.

"I mean, it was really a tiny town way out in the boonies," he said as he dragged his bar stool closer to me. "There was just this one saloon in a great barn of a room. They must have used the room for dances and meetings when the people came in from the ranches. I'm sitting at the bar and everyone's looking at me. I tell you, I felt strange, stranger than usual. It's like I'm a man from Mars.

"What was I doing there? I was part of an advance cadre setting up this new camp for the Army. Way in the wilds of Idaho. I don't think it was even on a map. We passed through the town on our way to the base. I borrowed a Jeep and went back that night because it looked like something from another world.

"I tell you it was unreal. Those people—there must have been a dozen cowboys or ranchers or farmers or whatever they were—hung around me like I'd just come down from Mars in a space ship. Some even touched me.

"It was spooky. I couldn't believe that in this day and age there were people who'd never seen a black man. That's what you had in this corner of the great U. S. of A.

"They didn't spit on me, like I've was spit on in Hattiesburg. Didn't throw me off my bar stool like they did in Fort Bragg. Didn't crowd me off the sidewalk like in Virginia Beach."

His voice rose as he recited this litany, the crisp notes of Pete Fountain's clarinet rising in counterpoint.

"No," he shook his head. The clarinet barely breathed its notes. "No, they bought me drinks. They took turns buying me drinks. They watched me drink as if I were a bear in a zoo. After a while, I joined in the fun. I bought them drinks. The whole dammed bar got as drunk as soldiers on their first leave. It was wild. But I proved to them that I was human," he laughed. "A drunken black human being."

He swigged on the beer before him. Pete's Five went into their famous "Saints Go Marching In" and the bar erupted: men and women rose, stamped their feet, clapped their hands and wriggled their way around the tables. Alec looked at them with an air of acceptance: Hey, that's what you do when the music is great.

I'd met Alec at a meeting earlier that night. Something, some spark between us, made us agree to have a beer together when the meeting ended. If he'd been a woman it may have been love at first sight. I don't know what you call it with a man like Alec Jones. A burly man, thick neck rising out of wide shoulders, he looked like an athlete, a football player. But he wasn't. He shuffled gracelessly and flatfootedly when he walked, and when I got to know him better, I learned that he shunned all athletics. He had a close-shaven head that could have been modeled after the Egyptian kings I'd seen in exhibits at the Metropolitan Museum.

Alec was a writer. He worked for an organization protecting the rights of foreign-born radicals whom the federal government wanted to deport because of their views. He showed me some of his work, written with simplicity, directness and clarity. He was that kind of man: simple, direct, clear. I liked him more and more as the music played, as the beer flowed and the revelers danced. I think he felt the same way about me. Before Nick's Bar closed, we agreed to find an apartment and share the rent.

That was the start of a friendship closer than the relationships I had with my own brothers. We lived together for more than two years, and even when we were separated by geography and marriages, we were bonded. In some mysterious way there were invisible fibers that bound us, brain cells that intermingled, and musical notes and laughter that enveloped us. After work we went everywhere together: dinner, parties, meetings, movies, theater, hikes, bus rides on the open top of the Fifth Avenue double-deckers, ferry rides to Staten Island, drives up the Hudson River parkway. Sometimes with dates. Foursomes. Most of the time without. The burly plodding black man and the gangly awkward white man—an unlikely pair, the original odd couple.

We were together, as usual, the night Ethel and Julius Rosenberg were executed. We were part of a huge crowd gathered at the north end of Union Square waiting, hoping against hope that the President, the Attorney General, the Supreme Court, anybody, any power on earth would stop the switch.

Alec and I often had worked late at night in the office of the Rosenberg defense attorney as volunteers—typing briefs, running them off on the mimeograph machines, collating and stapling. Work that had to be done. There was no money in the defense committee with which to hire office workers, so we and many other volunteers pitched in night after night.

At sundown on the eve of the Sabbath that June night the crowd suddenly hushed and turned toward the west. The sun filtered over graying buildings, throwing shadows over the thousands in the square. A radio crackled the news. A collective wail—a fusing of terrible pain, anguish, sorrow, anger and rage—burst from thousands of throats. My eyes rained tears. I looked at Alec. Tears were streaming down his cheeks.

Men and women around us were locked together, arms around each other, some sobbing, some keening, some still screaming. I looked again at Alec. He nodded and flicked his head at me, a signal to go. We turned together and walked slowly away from the crowd. All traffic had halted or had been diverted from the street. We stumbled down the middle of the street together, blinded by the tears.

The sobbing did not subside as we walked from the square. It came right along with us. We turned and saw that the crowd was streaming behind us, stumbling and shuffling in ragged lines.

"Hey, what are we gonna do?" Alec said to me out of the side of his mouth. "We're the leaders here."

I shrugged and shook my head. I was too full of shock and bitterness to talk. Who gave a damn, anyway?

Alec looked back at the crowd behind us—hundreds of people, weeping hysterically, clinging to each other, keeping each other from falling to the street. He took my arm and gently pulled me along. He turned left at Fifth Avenue, and the crowd followed us down the middle of the street. Cars slowed and pulled aside. Cops stared at us and then directed traffic around the line of mourners now stretching for many blocks behind us.

Alec didn't say a word. His head was rigid and fixed. His eyes had a determined, angry look. His lips were clamped together. He set each foot down before him as if he were stamping his tracks on a beach. I don't know how he did it, but suddenly I looked up and we were in front of the huge apartment complex that had been the Rosenbergs' home before their arrest.

The crowd gathered at an intersection, shutting off traffic four ways. Quietly, almost silently, as if in prayer, the mourners clung together, blocking out the cacophony of horns that came from cars stalled on the streets. Then, sadly, dejectedly, they pulled away from each other and went to their homes, to their neighborhood bar, to a friend's, to a hole in the ground, to who knows where you go when you are battered, hurt and defeated.

Alec said his feet took him to the Rosenberg home. "My mind wasn't working."

THERE WERE GIRLFRIENDS in both our lives. We entertained many in our small one-bedroom apartment on the top floor of an old building in the Chelsea section of Manhattan. We were both pretty good cooks; we'd ply the women with exotic culinary delights such as paella, provide plenty of wine and loud talk, wild stories, political diatribes, joyous laughter. It was the freedom of a couple of bachelors, not at all like the freedom and loneliness of one bachelor.

We'd both suffered painful divorces, and the hurts were beginning to heal. Our coming together was part of the healing. So were the dates and parties. Life was joyful again.

Until Mona came. Young, blond and beautiful, somewhat wild and defiant, she fell in love with Alec. The daughter of a Communist labor leader, she'd been brought up to accept the naturalness of white-black relationships. She'd grown up with many black friends in the cooperative apartments in the Bronx where she'd been born and raised, and had had black boyfriends among her many dates.

Ordinarily a considerate, thoughtful man, Alec became even more considerate of Mona's needs and desires and could not do enough for this sweet, buxom college sophomore whose blond hair was carelessly fluffed and curled. She looked as if she were still in high school, but her steely grey eyes missed nothing, and made you realize that Mona knew what she was doing at all times.

Mona would cut classes to watch us concoct a meal in the kitchen and have dinner with us. She told her mother and father that she was studying in the library and would leave our apartment to return home late at night, when the library closed. Her grades suffered. And she became pregnant.

The three of us sat in the small living room one night discussing Mona and Alec's problem. All sides of it, with many drinks to ease the talk and worry.

Finally, after taking a long sip on bourbon, Alec said: "The solution is simple. Mona will you have me in marriage? Will you be my bride?"

Those were his words.

Mona, with a big, beautiful smile, was caught up in Alec's courtliness. She replied, "Oh, yes, my beautiful lover. With all my heart." They embraced. And went to bed.

What to do next? Elope? Have a small wedding with friends? Tell Mona's mother and father and get their blessing for a larger wedding? In any case, Mona's parents had to be told. Mona made the trip back to the Bronx with trepidation.

Mother and father blew up in anger—especially father, the old-line Bolshevik. He argued that Mona was too young. She hadn't finished school. She wasn't prepared for life. He'd raised her—an only child—to be an independent woman, not a housewife. And besides, Alec was black. Her children would be black. Society didn't accept "miscegenation." Society mistreated children of mixed marriages. And the white wives of black men.

Mona called tearfully to report. She wasn't allowed out of the house. Alec took two or three glasses of bourbon after each call.

But Mona didn't tell her parents about being pregnant. I don't know what their reaction would have been if she had. That was a problem Alec and she dealt with.

Both became resigned to the impossibility of their marriage, Mona because she did not, or could not, oppose her parents, Alec because he did not want to force Mona to oppose them.

They went off one afternoon. When they returned, Mona leaned heavily on Alec's arm. She walked slowly through the apartment to the bedroom, sniffling. Alec looked grim. A short while later she went to the bathroom and stayed for what seemed like hours. Alec leaned against the bathroom door, saying "Are you okay, Mona? Are you okay?"

Mona finally unlocked the door and walked out. "Look," she said. Alec went to the toilet and looked down. He called me. I stood behind him and saw a small mass of blood in the bowl. "That's the fetus," Alec said, and turned away. I flushed the toilet. He couldn't.

Alec was never the same after that. He began to drink much more heavily than usual: a bottle of cheap bourbon a day. Perhaps it was because of his disappointment over a marriage that never materialized, or the fetus flushed into New York's sewers. Perhaps it was his feeling about Mona's father, who represented the staunch Communist philosophy Alec admired. Alec had become a Communist because he wanted a society that accepted him, that was not racist, that would permit people of all color and persuasions to flower. He felt betrayed.

Not only had his love for Mona been denied him by a Communist leader who espoused love for all mankind, but it had been done in a brutal, racist fashion. What then was the difference between a racist and a Communist Party member? The degree of openness? Racists hated openly. Communists talked against racism and hated secretly.

We talked about it, Alec sharing his bottle with me. His anger and bitterness grew with each drink as we each grappled with an evil we hadn't realized was so pervasive.

So began a slow suicide. Alec was in a drunken stupor most of the afternoon and evening. He'd fall into bed when the bottle emptied, rouse himself early in the morning, walk to work a few blocks away, and rush home in the early afternoon with a brown paper sack holding the bourbon.

I was away from the apartment a good part of the time, involved with Joyce, a woman I'd met at an Easter party. I tried to spend time with Alec, but he shut the door on me, hiding in the bedroom with his whiskey. Joyce and I cooked some of the food he liked and set it out for him. He turned it all away.

My high school buddy, Paul, had introduced me to Joyce at the party. She was a friend of Paul's girlfriend. Joyce and I hit it off immediately and stayed up all night long talking, swapping life stories in a White Castle restaurant, eating dime hamburgers and drinking nickel coffees.

She was very pretty, and despite hefty buttocks—which she described as 'scholar's butt'—very agile, light and quick on her feet, especially when she tap-danced. She worked as an instructor in philosophy at Barnard College while she pursued her Ph.D. at Columbia. She was quick with the rejoinder, tenacious in debate—captain of the University of Michigan debate team for two years—and the most articulate person I'd ever met. We went together for months, until school ended for the summer. She returned to her home in Los Angeles, and when Barnard resumed classes in the fall I proposed to her. I asked Alec to be my best man at the wedding. He sobered up and stood beside me as the rabbi conducted the ceremony. Then he got drunk at the wedding party, an appropriate time. People should always get drunk at weddings.

I moved into an apartment with my new wife, Joyce. Alec was alone again. No Mona. No me. Just Good Ole U.S.A. Rotgut and Universal Red Racist Hatred as companions.

I left New York for Los Angeles with Joyce and lost touch with Alec for several years, immersed in my own problems of finding and holding a job, of fixing up an old house, and of helping take care of a new baby.

I heard about him through New York friends, who said that he had a job in the national mail order department of J.C. Penney Company. He'd married the widow of a famous playwright. He was completely sober.

WHEN I SAW ALEC AGAIN on a visit to New York years later, he told me how he'd sobered up. Drunk one night, Alec drove a car down a street and blindly rammed into other cars. It was a resolving incident; he vowed to cure his sickness. He moved into an apartment with a seaman who shipped out on long voyages.

When his roommate went to sea, Alec lugged boxes of canned and frozen food from a supermarket to his apartment. He locked and bolted his door, poured every drop of alcohol into the toilet, pulled the shades, took the phone off the hook, and sat back in bed. He put a Do Not Disturb sign on his door and didn't respond to any knocks.

The first few weeks without a drink, he said, were nightmarish. He shook endlessly. He beat his head against the apartment walls and screamed into a pillow in his pain. He tossed endlessly in bed and couldn't sleep. He propped himself against the bathtub and stretched out on the tile floor to relieve his fever. He stripped himself naked to cool off. He wanted to pull his skin off, he said, to break the fever. He was chilled, and couldn't wear enough clothes or cover himself with enough blankets to stop the shivering. He lost all taste for food and couldn't eat for weeks. He drank water—gallons of it—and had visions that he was drinking whiskey. The visions brought dreams of rooms full of bugs and snakes—the classic D.T.'s.

Gradually, after weeks of anguish, the visions diminished, the tremors abated, the appetite returned, the shades went up and light came back into the apartment. It took Alec almost two months to rid his body of the poison that had been devouring him.

I'd never heard of a more courageous action in my life, and told him so. He shrugged and said, "It had to be done. I couldn't have gone on living." He made it sound easy.

I also learned from friends that Mona's parents made sure she got as far away from Alec as possible. They sent her to school in Italy. She completed her university training and was admitted to medical school, later receiving her degree and beginning practice in a hospital, specializing in pediatrics.

Barbara, the widow Alec had married, was introduced to him by his half-sister, who I never knew existed. Alec had been born and raised in Milwaukee; his half-sister, Fran, in Boston. They didn't know of each other's existence until their father died. A Pullman porter on the Milwaukee to Boston Line, Alec's father kept a family at each end of his run. It was uncanny, but Alec and Fran looked like twins.

I met Fran years later in the hospital in New York, where Alec was being treated for colon cancer. Fran was seated at his bedside when I tiptoed into the room. She recognized me, though I'd never seen her in my life.

"Alec talked about you all the time. He described you down to a 't.' I'd know you anywhere," she said, her voice low. "I don't know why I'm whispering. Force of habit, I guess. He can't hear us. He's sedated and he just had chemotherapy. That always knocks him out."

She was a smaller, female version of Alec. The same high forehead, hair cropped tightly around a noble head, long, rounded jaw and teeth that glinted in frequent smiles.

"And you're the spittin' image of Alec," I said. I felt comfortable, as if I were talking to Alec.

We sat beside the bed for a while. I watched Alec—immobile, his breathing indiscernible, his eyes tightly shut and his arms rigid at his sides.

"I'm giving Barbara a break," Fran explained. Alec didn't move in the hour we sat talking. Fran occasionally patted beads of sweat from his forehead. When Barbara finally appeared, she hugged me and looked anxiously at Alec. She was blonde, her hair windblown and free around an oval, full face.

"He's not doing so good today," she said, as if afraid that he might hear. "The pain was too much for him—they doped him pretty heavily." She leaned over to stroke his hand.

"He can't talk, and he can hardly hear, and that frustrates him so much. But he can feel my touch and he can see. So I hold his hand all the time. He'll be so glad to see you." She caressed Alec's hand. "Here," she said. "You do it."

I rubbed Alec's hand—brown, with little black wisps of hair above the broad knuckles and along the wrist. I rubbed gently, with all the tenderness I had within me, with all the love I could muster. Maybe I could rub out the pain and disease. Maybe I could stay the switch.

And so I sat beside the bed, my hand on Alec's, Barbara on one side, Fran on the other, and we talked about a friend, brother, lover and husband. All the same man. All different men.

We sat in the hushed, darkening room, the rustle of the hospital shut out by the closed door. Alec's hand stirred in mine. It fumbled along the bed sheet and his body twitched. When his eyes opened and tried to focus in the dark, Barbara turned on a lamp attached to the bed. Alec's eyes swiveled from Fran to Barbara and me.

Barbara took his hand and, shouting into his ear, said, "It's Mel. He came all the way from California."

She didn't have to shout. He knew who it was. His eyes fixed on me. He was trying to tell me something with his eyes. Two rivers of tears welled up and broke down his cheeks. I felt tears on my own cheeks, our lives commingled in tears.

EPILOGUE

B etween the winter of 1952 and the winter of 2000, when I write this epilogue, I passed through many springtimes. Somehow, the jonquils and daffodils always thrust themselves up from the cold hard earth and led me to new friends, new lovers, new directions and vistas.

To be sure, there were other hard winters, but the springtimes always came.

I had several futile jobs in the Communist movement: publicity director and writer of a weekly newsletter for the "second-string Communists" on trial in New York. Slinging a pebble against the governmental Goliath. I wrote press releases and pamphlets for the Civil Rights Congress, slinging more pebbles.

I'd moved to jobs on magazines by the time I married Joyce, and had to resign from one when the editor asked me to swear that I was "not now and never had been a Communist," the oath in vogue then. So I was unemployed when our son, Daniel, was born May 12, 1956.

The sudden death of my father on an operating table—along with the frustration of six months of free-lance writing and job-hunting—convinced us that we had to get out of New York.

My father, suffering from bleeding ulcers, was advised by my Uncle Alex's son-in-law, a doctor, to have them operated on. Weakened by months of poor diet and bleeding, my father's heart stopped moments after the incision into his stomach was made. In the hospital waiting room, we were crushed by the news: the suddenness, the improbability, the finality. Years later, medical science determined that bleeding ulcers were caused by bacteria, not by growths on the stomach lining.

Joyce cashed in some of her war bond savings for plane tickets to Los Angeles, where her parents lived. There, I knocked on the doors of dozens of newspapers in the sprawling area and found one interested publisher.

He called me in August, when we had returned to New York, and asked me to take over his paper. My mother financed a small new Ford. I hooked on a trailer, loaded it with our belongings, and with Daniel in a back seat crib, we steamed across the country to Torrance, an industrial suburb south of Los Angeles.

For five months I edited a weekly paper. The publisher then decided the paper was so good it should be produced twice weekly. My work doubled. I asked for a raise. He added $25 to my $500 a month. He was shocked when I told him what to do with the $25.

I finally found another editing and writing job on a magazine called *Popular Ceramics*, a monthly catering to hobbyists. Five years later, Joyce and I started our own magazine aimed at manufacturers and distributors of supplies to hobbyists. We produced *Ceramic Scope* first from our bedroom, then from our backyard garage, and finally from an office building we purchased a few blocks from our home after the magazine prospered.

Prosperity was welcomed, because our family had been enlarged by the birth of Jessica on June 5, 1960. The good times also enabled Joyce to become active in the American Civil Liberties Union (ACLU) and, after a few years, to be elected the first woman president of the local chapter.

But during that time, despite the satisfaction of being independent, running a successful magazine, hiring a half-dozen people, and paying enormous printing bills, I felt the magazine to be a granite boulder barring my way from some other vague vision I had of myself. It was a burden. And Joyce, too, became someone who restricted me, who overcame me with her brilliance, her unceasing flow of words.

We went through trying sessions with therapists, psychologists, marriage counselors. I went on four- and five-hour walks on beaches or in parks. Agonizing. Thinking. Ruminating.

Finally, I left Joyce. A wrenching, ghastly experience. Moved into my own apartment in Playa del Rey, a Los Angeles beach town, and sold the magazine. My burdens were lifted.

I retired, started writing my memoirs, and became active in organizations such as the Office of the Americas, which in 1985 became one of the sponsors of an International March for Peace in Central America. I was one of the marchers—some 350 from thirty-three countries. We flew into Panama City, where a camp used by agricultural workers was reserved for our tent city. From there we went on buses to Costa Rica, which at first denied us entrance because we were accused of being Communist emissaries. On the border, I slept on the loading dock of a filthy customs house until we were permitted to enter Costa Rica. In San Jose, the capital, we were driven out by tear gas and rock barrages flung by state-sponsored youth groups.

I became violently ill when we reached Nicaragua. I couldn't continue the march and flew back to Los Angeles just before Christmas, four weeks after I'd left. It took me a year to get rid of the jungle parasite I'd picked up. The marchers went on, flying over Honduras, which had barred them, to Guatemala, then by bus to a triumphant welcome in Mexico City.

Just before I left Los Angeles for the march, I'd written Diana Farnham, my former wife, now Diana O'Hehir, applauding her new book, *I Wish This War Were Over,* which had been nominated for a Pulitzer Prize. She wrote that she would be delighted to autograph a copy of the book for me. I mailed a copy, which she signed and returned. I thanked her and said I owed her a beer. She replied that I owed her a dinner.

Several weeks after my return from Nicaragua, I drove to Berkeley and bought her a dinner of Maryland crab cakes. Blonde, trim and still striking and sparkling, she greeted me with a warmth and effusiveness that belied thirty-six years of separation.

That was in 1986. We've been together ever since—an ardent, accepting attachment. And I became step-father to her son, Andrew.

(Diana has written a memoir of our marriage and reconciliation, called *Burn, Bridges, Burn.*)

Together we've watched our children grow in maturity, self-respect and achievement: Andrew as a playwright, movie critic and budding novelist; Michael becoming absorbed in the study of chiropractic medicine; Jessica, happily married, advancing to a rewarding job on the University of California campus in Berkeley, and Daniel as publisher and co-editor of a legal magazine, *Verdict,* the publication of his organization, the Coalition of Concerned Legal Professionals. They haven't, as yet, produced any grandchildren.

I still see Joe and George of *The Argonauts* when I return to New York. Lillian writes occasionally. Helen died in 1971. In 1989 I proposed a reunion and a return trip. I was rebuffed, even though I wasn't interested in the same broad examination of America we'd undertaken fifty years earlier. I preferred a narrow look at ourselves. Had we found the Golden Fleece?

That's still a good question, one each of us has to answer: Lillian as a famous staff writer for *The New Yorker*; George as chairman of the board of a big corporation; and Joe as a long-time colleague of Ed Murrow and a producer for *60 Minutes.*

As for me, I may have held the Golden Fleece briefly at some time in my life. I may have viewed my dreams of social justice, of an end to poverty and hunger, of housing for all, of a more equitable life for everyone as steps to grasping the Fleece. I may have touched the Fleece on one of my numerous jobs, or held it when I embraced one of the women I loved and married. I may have seen it in the faces of my newborn children, may have captured it in some of the millions of words I wrote, may have clasped hands with the Fleece through the friends I made from childhood on. Will I ever know if and when I've ever had the Fleece in my grasp?

And what happened to my America during that search? Hunger and poverty still exist, hidden but pervasive. The chasm between the poor and the rich has grown wider and deeper. The Hoovervilles of the

Depression have been supplanted by a shifting, growing core of displaced, homeless people who live out of shopping carts. A standing army of police and prison guards keeps a restless underclass under constant surveillance and behind bars. The nation's wealth is being squandered on deadly weapons and endless wars, unholy alliances with Hitlerian dictators, and on intelligence agencies whose aim is control and power. America's government—from city halls to state houses to Congress to the Presidency—has been sold to the highest bidders, the ever-more-powerful corporate conglomerates and multinationals. But most telling is the great disillusionment—about voting, about politicians, about government—spread across the land.

It pains me, today, years after I left the Party, to see how little of our work is left standing. The labor movement has been decimated by business opposition and government antagonism. The fervor of the Party to better life for the people—to look after our children and neighbors—has been choked off. After years of fierce anti-Communist wars, the Party and its influence has been wiped from the face of the nation. The Party is now—as it was then—considered an evil that had to be obliterated. Its members had to be destroyed; the memory of their existence suppressed.

The fierceness of the anti-Communist war was brought home to me when—after three years of argument, implorings, supplications and letters from me and congresspeople and senators—the FBI sent 872 pages of their files on me. I understand now why they were so reluctant to release them. Those files expose the ineptness, stupidity and ignorance of the regiments of agents who day after day for years sought to harass and suppress the Communists. They reveal the FBI's illegalities, lies and fairy tales.

We were no danger to anyone. We couldn't even organize ourselves, much less a country for "revolution." We were lucky in the '30's when workers, fed up with Depression, hunger and poverty, joined together to form militant unions. The Communists were right there along with the workers in steel, auto and mines. In the 40's and 50's, the Communists were isolated by the Truman-McCarthy attacks. *Defend us,* the Party cried hysterically to the workers. But the people had more important things to do, such as rebuilding their lives after World War II, making babies, and supporting families.

I remained in the Party until 1956 because I kept telling myself that I would not be cowed by the FBI, Truman, or McCarthy. I wouldn't let the bastards grind me down. But when Stalin invaded Hungary and his tyrannical rule was exposed by Khrushchev, I realized that I had not been living in the real world.

I was called all kinds of names, spit on, cursed, stalked, harassed—but I survived many of the agents, politicians, bureaucrats, police, spies and detractors who considered me an enemy. I insisted on my right to believe whatever I wanted and to associate with whom I wanted—rights guaranteed to me under our Constitution. As a native-born son of two naturalized citizens I certainly was entitled to all the constitutional rights of a citizen.

And I gave as a citizen: three years in the Marines, a taxpayer for more years than I can count, a voter who never missed an election, a worker, an employer, a member of fact-finding commissions and neighborhood planning boards, a protester in front of city halls, a marcher with anti-Vietnam contingents, a writer of letters to elected officials and to editors. In short, a red-blooded living, breathing American.

My problem was that I believed the system should be changed so that the poor would get richer and the rich get poorer. I believed that the mountains of money and power held by the rich should be leveled off into the hollows, ghettos, barrios and skid rows in which the poor—white, black, tan and red—live. Is that so terrible?

I didn't think so then. I still don't today.

0-595-24001-1